Marketing Design using AI

By Neal Hettinger

FlintGroup
PUBLISHERS

Editor: Sheryl Ralston

Cover design: D. Hettinger.

ISBN 979-8-9929481-1-0 | Paperback

Genre: Marketing Design

COM100000 COMPUTERS / Artificial Intelligence / Generative AI *

DES007050 DESIGN / Graphic Arts / Typography

BUS043010 BUSINESS & ECONOMICS / Marketing / Direct

Printed in the United States of America.

FlintGroup

PUBLISHERS

flintpublishers.com

Foreword

I am a guy who thought AI was a steak sauce! Neal has written a step-by-step understanding that even I can grasp and use. He emphasizes how to use AI technology for results. He provides multiple examples of prompts and shows how different AI generators solve them.

Entrepreneurs don't want to learn how the watch is built when they ask what time it is!

You, like me, want straight-to-the-point answers. How can this help me in my business? What do I have to know?

For over twenty years, I have depended on Neal Hettinger (HDG) to provide me the shortest, most useful answers on how to keep my company up with future technologies. My company is the most visible property inspection company in the southwest due to his marketing design, software creation, and team learning techniques.

BRAVO, Neal, and THANK YOU! The book is excellent, providing sufficient information for a novice like me, particularly in the area of social media posting.

—Jack Werner, PhD, Owner, A to Z Inspections

Acknowledgments

Thank you to every one of my friends, family, and business owners for discussing their AI requirements with me. Jack Werner, PhD, was a terrific sounding board for thoughts on how AI may be applied in housing, and he graciously prepared a brief introduction.

I met Courtney Oliphant, a librarian, at her AI workshop where she showed me some of the AI tools she uses, like Goblin. I recognized the potential it could have as an AI marketing campaign planner.

Mike Soto has a thriving floor installation company, and one of his innovative ideas for gaining work is to develop relationships with plumbers, roofers, home inspectors, and painters. They were frequently working on homes that could benefit from Mike's services, and he would also refer them. This turned into an idea for how to gain more followers.

Sarah Strawn was the experienced Realtor® who came up with the strong concept of selling a house by presenting something unique rather than just showing the exterior. Sidney and Will Blake, founders of Vesta Foundation Solutions, demonstrated their uncommon marketing plan to me. They presented their competitor's smaller pier next to their larger Vesta pier. That was a strong presentation.

I truly appreciate the time and effort Sheryl, my wife, put into my manuscript. She enjoys reading about topics that fascinate her, but I know AI in design is not at the top of her list.

Preface

This book is for innovative marketers, tech-savvy business owners, and graphic designers to learn about the available AI generative tools and ways to use them. Cost-conscious business owners are already creating promotional pieces for themselves or hiring someone online for less than the price of a haircut to create their company's communications. Now they can turn their ideas into professional, effective marketing, adding value to their brands.

Marketers and graphic designers need to learn the AI tools. They will be able to create designs in multiple styles without having to hire illustrators, photographers, and video editors to save them time and stay up-to-date with the latest trends.

With an academic background that includes a Master of Arts degree in Mass Communications and a Bachelor of Arts degree in Graphic Arts with a minor in English, teaching was in my future. But first I needed real-world experience, which I received at design firms and advertising agencies in Los Angeles, Nashville, Oklahoma City, and Birmingham. I was fortunate to have a varied client list that included Nissan Motors, Universal Studios, Paramount Pictures, and adidas.

Publications such as The New York Times have quoted me, and I have written articles for various print magazines as well as numerous online journals and websites. My firm specializes in graphic design marketing, visual websites, UX software, and UI workflow platforms. As a professor, I received a tremendous honor by being presented with the Outstanding Faculty Award from OCCC.

Teaching and passing on the knowledge I have gained through experience is rewarding. Especially when a student sees how to be creative.

Contents

This book is intended to help creatives with AI—not to replace marketers and designers.

Those professionals have the education, training, experience, and knowledge of the best strategies to place your company at the next level of success.

Enjoy designing—it is fun!

Introduction of artificial intelligence

1

Learning objectives

The learner will recall AI generative terms, and they will understand how copyright law applies to AI generated images and designs. The reader will be able to use marketing acronyms and professional terminology.

Marketers are creative

As a graphic artist, professor, and author, I chose to teach marketers and business owners how to design marketing materials using AI generative tools. Some graphic designers disapprove of this approach. However, creativity is essential for everyone in these fields. With current technology, it is possible to explain the basics to anyone who doesn't want to attend art school or college to create simple designs.

There are graphic designers who create and plan marketing campaigns. Many marketing and advertising firms whose owners are graphic designers. The reason a few graphic designers dislike the idea of teaching individuals how to use artificial intelligence generative tools is because the creatives will not know what good graphic design is supposed to accomplish. There are plenty of weak solutions by graphic designers.

Not long ago, a person could not be a graphic artist unless they able to draw, paint, and capture an image photographically.

Computers with design software and mobile phones with cameras changed that notion. As a side note, the mobile phone image uses the equivalent of a 24mm lens. The standard digital camera uses 50mm lens so the images are tremendously better but it is not easy to lug around. If given the choice, use a digital camera for taking pictures.

AI is giving creative-minded professionals the ability to compose visual designs. If people are taught the tools, then it is better for everyone in the visual communication fields.

IMAGE 1-1

AI Practicum | Adobe Firefly prompt: Create an image of an AI content generator in a computer glowing and having magical stars coming out.

AI content generators

Artificial intelligence offers accessible and helpful writing tools. When you write and want to review your composition, you can paste it into AI assistants. Many online writing apps offer desktop versions such as Word and QuillBot.

Research all the available free and paid options. Besides finding misspellings, they can find grammatical errors, suggest ways to improve the wording, summarize long texts, paraphrase and simplify long awkward content, and improve concepts.

AI content generators can take your phrases and create content and brainstorm potential ideas. Predictive text is another form of AI assistance when you message or email.

You should always proof the content for accuracy and plagiarism. AI is a strong writing tool but does not replace a human for creativity and high-quality writing. A recent Futurism online magazine article reported that many of the AI results are incorrect. They tested eight AI generators, such as ChatGPT and Google's Gemini, and found that over 60% of the queries had the incorrect answers.[1]

Structure of prompts

This book is focused on using AI tools for image and marketing generation. Lectures and classes on how to create effective prompts can be found at your local library and online. The structure and details of prompts vary by each AI generator, but once you use one, a pattern and structure can become evident.

An overview

When speaking with marketers and businesspeople, I discovered that many of them posted a lot with the impression that they were branding their company. Most of them did not have time to do more than put up something about their latest project. However, when I posed the question, if no one sees or remembers your post, why are you wasting your time? The answer was they felt they needed to do something. This book was written to allow you to create social posts that will stand out, be memorable, and make people interested enough to pause and see your post. It also has details such as when is the best time to post based on the platform and which platform is the best for your product or service.

Marketers also create basic marketing pieces such as flyers, postcards, and rack cards. This book covers how to apply AI generative tools to these designs. If you need to know the minute details, then you should probably hire a graphic designer. If you know how to set up a file with crops and bleeds and know that print uses CMYK inks, then you may find the information beneficial.

While it is recommended to read the entire book from start to finish, this overview can help you quickly locate specific subjects without having to search through every page. An index is in the back for topics, words, and phrases.

There are 14 chapters in this book, which is not enough to explain every single detail of marketing design. This book is an abbreviated version of marketing principles and execution strategies that utilize time-tested methods and time-saving AI-generated processes. The goal is to teach the basics so that a creative marketer, who does not have the time to hire a professional graphic designer, can create solutions on their own. The content is geared for small business owners who do not have the budget to hire a professional for all of the company's branding.

To design a professional-appearing post and collateral marketing is not difficult when a creative person learns the basics and how to apply the tricks of the trade. Some design areas you should spend the time and money on a professional designer. A logo, for instance, needs to be readable at all sizes. Yet at least half of the self-designed solutions are not very good. You should contract a graphic artist to design expensive advertising campaigns. The company is spending a great deal of money, so don't cut corners.

Many times, something occurs that warrants a quick turnaround mailer. You may want something that you can put into a door so when someone comes home, they can see it. Perhaps you want something you can leave behind in a restaurant. It is a quick read placed so that someone could read while they wait to be seated. There are a lot of marketing ways to promote your company, industry, or service, and they are not expensive to produce with online printing. You can save a lot of money if you use an existing template that comes with print shops and with AI apps such as Adobe Express and Canva. You start with the same template everyone else is using, but you create something unique to make it memorable.

At the beginning of each chapter are Learning Objectives. This lets you know the focus of the chapter and is used for a quick reference when you are trying to find something you have read in this book.

Throughout each chapter, you will see images, most of which were created with artificial intelligence generators. Instead of taking you through the multitude of artificial intelligence generators, many of which are listed in Chapter 14, AI Practicums are shown below the images.

Each Practicum identifies how the image was created with AI and includes a callout of the name of the artificial intelligence generator used along with the wording for the prompt. This wording is a short explanation or description used by the AI platform to obtain the image that created the image shown.

An interesting phenomenon occurs with AI generators. An individual can enter a prompt one day, and when they go back on another day and enter the same prompt in the same generator, they get a different solution.

Updates will have occurred since the publication of this book, as is the case with any technology. The progress in AI is accelerating at a rapid pace. Frequently, artificial intelligence generators are available online for free, with free trial periods, and the majority require subscriptions. You are strongly encouraged to experiment with them for various marketing initiatives prior to enrolling.

Copyrighting AI-generated designs

When using generative AI tools for creating images and designs, the results are generally available for commercial purposes. According to the US Copyright Office (see below), copyright ownership cannot be claimed for any of the images. AI-generated images may infringe on third-party intellectual property rights. Please review the "Generative AI Terms of Use" for any AI tools you utilize.

The US Copyright Office has confirmed that AI-generated material and suggestions are not protected by copyright. In its report, Copyright and Artificial Intelligence, Part 2: Copyrightability, the office concluded that "Copyright protects the original expression in a work created by a human author, even if the work also includes AI-generated material."

Conversely, copyright does not apply to AI-generated content that includes some human content. The report clarified that from a graphic design standpoint, artificial intelligence is copyrightable if it is used as a tool to style or produce effects in human-generated work.

For definitive guidance on your design, consult a copyright attorney. The report is available at: copyright.gov/ai/Copyright-and-Artificial-Intelligence-Part-2-Copyrightability-Report.pdf

IMAGE 1-2

AI Practicum | Google Gemini prompt: Create an image of a marketer speaking to a businessman with financial posters in the background. Note the fingers are correct, and they do not have too many eyes.

99 in marketing terms

The 99 in marketing is a popular number. It is a pricing strategy based on how potential customers will look at the first numbers of the cost of a service or product and feel that it is lower than if the price was rounded up. $1199.99 is less expensive than $1200.00. It is simple, but it works.

To work in the industry and discuss projects with professionals, you will need to know the language or at least have this quick source to find the terms. Fellow marketers, graphic designers, artists, developers, and printers will gauge your experience and education by how well you understand and use industry verbiage. Social media, websites, and printers have specs and guidelines that you must follow, but you need to understand the terms.

Throughout the book, words will be used that are either not explained or are defined only once. If you miss the explanation, you can refer to this chapter. For experienced marketers and designers, when professional terminology is used, they will not have to wade through the definition each time.

IMAGE 1-3

AI Practicum | Microsoft Creator prompt: create an image of a 99¢ in 3 dimension floating over a stack of money. Note the money is not very exact and blurred.

Many readers will skip around in the chapters looking for a specific item they are interested in at that time. Instead of repeating the definition in each chapter where it is used or explaining the term, the term should be found in the following list. You will remember the verbiage better by looking it up here and not have to reread the explanation every time it is used in subsequent chapters.

Marketers love to use acronyms since they want to keep all communication short and to the point, so do not feel uneducated if you need to look them up here. This industry terminology refers to artificial intelligence generative tools, graphic design, marketing, social posting, and printing.[2]

Industry terms

Advertisement: A paid message promoting a product, service, or event.

Aesthetics: The arrangement of elements in a design to be harmonious.

Artificial Intelligence: A mechanical intelligence that simulates human intelligence to execute visual and verbal solutions.

Balance: Where the visual weight of a layout's elements is harmonious.

Body Copy: Content in paragraph form that communicates the message

BOGO: Buy one—get one free.

Brand: A visual identification system that distinguishes a company, app, or business.

CTA: Call to action verbiage that inspires the reader to react in a particular way.

Calligraphy: Freehand lettering, usually with a pen or brush, that can be decorative.

Carousel: A single ad that allow multiple images, or videos.

Character: The letters that make up a typeface.

Chatbot: An application that communicates with humans through text.

Client: The person hiring the services of a graphic designer.

CMYK: For print, cyan, magenta, yellow, and black inks are used and printed in this order.

Complementary colors: Opposite hues on the color wheel producing contrast in designs.

Content: Verbiage in a design.

Contrast: Visually different elements that attract a person's attention.

Cool color: Hues on the color wheel mixed with blue.

Copy: Words combined to convey a message or piece of information.

Critique: An evaluation with positive and negative feedback.

CRM: Customer Relationship Management assists businesses in utilizing their customer data and interactions.

Demographics: The statistical characteristics of the audience

Design: The creative composition of elements to create a message.

Direct mail: Postcards and flyers manually delivered by a postal service to potential customers.

Door hanger: Door handle- or knob-mounted printed marketing.

Draft: Ideas that need editing for grammar and spelling before publication.

EEDM®: Marketing is delivered by the USPS to every residence within a zip code.

Face: A specific font design based on structure.

File: The digital collection of data stored by name and extension.

Filigree: Delicate ornamental dividers and borders formed to break up content and space.

Font: A collection of characters with a specific face and size.

Foreshortening: Shortening or distorting an object to give the illusion of depth.

Format: Size, shape, and use of the design in print, motion graphics, or the internet.

Generate: Using the information supplied to produce a potential solution.

Generative AI: Technology that creates text, video, or images with artificial intelligence from a human prompt.

Graphic: A designed visual element.

Hero image: A large, impactful visual that usually fills most of the post or website page.

Hi-res: An image quality suitable for printing.

Hierarchy: Elements are ranked by importance.

Hue: The name of a color.

Identity: The brand's visual individuality designed for consumer recognition.

Image: A visual representation of a form in photography, illustration, or painting.

Intensity: The saturation and visual strength of color.

Keyword: A word or a phrase internet users use in a search engine query.

K.I.S.S.: Keep it simple, short.

KPI: Key Performance Indicators that track traffic, conversion rates, and engagements.

Icon: An abstract or literal graphic element used to represent an object or action.

Leave behind: Post-sales pitch flyers remind prospects of the proposal.

Legible: A recognizable communication.

Letterspace: The kerning or tracking of letters in a word.

Logo: A uniquely designed graphic to represent an entity that establishes the brand.

Lowercase: Shorter non-capital letters with ascenders and descenders to improve readability.

Marketing: A strategic plan to promote a brand's service, event, or product.

Menu: A list of options for narrowing down results.

Meta: Verbiage that describes an element's content.

Mood Board: A collection of references, such as images and textures, to incorporate in a design.

Narrative: A created story or message.

Palette: Compiling colors as part of the strategy for a design.

PMS colors: Pantone Matching System special inks that have a broader range of colors but are a more expensive system since it requires exact parts to be mixed to obtain a color.

Paraphrase: Rewording phrases or sentences without losing their meaning.

Pattern: An arrangement of a repeated decoration or ornament in design.

PDF: Portable Document Format is a cross-platform file that displays a document without the data that generated it.

Photoshop: Adobe tool for digitally editing, retouching, and manipulating an image.

Pillars: Consistent concepts that hold the campaign together and support each element.

Pixel: Bits of visual information that together compose images or communication.

Primary colors: The top three hues of the color wheel that cannot be obtained by mixing other colors.

Prompt: Inputs that direct the AI tools in a direction to produce a solution.

Rack card: Marketing for foot traffic located on holders.

Readable: Type that is easy to interpret and quickly understand.

Resolution: The quantity of pixels used to produce an image.

RGB: Amounts of red, green, and blue lights on a monitor, television, movie screen, and electronic devices where the image is created with a combination of color lighting.

Roman: Letterforms that are vertical and horizontal and not slanted or sloping.

S.M.A.R.T.: A marketing goal that is Specific, Measurable, Attainable, Realistic, and Time-Specific.

Sales: Presenting a service or product for purchase to a potential customer.

Scalable: Able to be changed in size, mode, and shape for different media.

Secondary color: Hues created by mixing primary colors.

Search generative experience: Results summarized by AI from Google searches.

Shade: Making a color darker, usually by adding black.

Space: The area around the placed design components that draws the viewer's focus.

Specs: Measurements of width and height with image resolution and color mode.

Target Market: A description of the customer group marketing is directed to interest.

Tertiary color: Hues created by mixing primary and secondary colors.

Text: A group of written or printed words to form a message or communication.

Texture: The tactile quality that creates a sensation of a consistency on a surface.

Tint: Making a color lighter, usually by adding white.

Tradeshow: An event where companies display their goods and services to potential clients.

Trifold: A marketing piece that folds twice, creating 6 panels.

Typeface: A set of designed characters created as an alphabet, punctuation, and glyphs.

Unique: Absolutely one of a kind.

USP: Unique Selling Proposition.

URL: Uniform Resource Locator is a browser address used to access websites and files.

Values: Lights and darks in an image.

Vintage: Signifying or having to do with something of quality from the past.

Visuals: A graphic design term indicating all the elements and components that can be seen.

Voice: How the communication is expressed through point of view or tone.

Warm color: Hues on the color wheel that are mixed with red or yellow.

White Space: The absence of any elements in an area of the design, including hues.

X-height: An invisible line that determines the height of a lowercase letter.

Zip: Compressing one or more digital files.

1 | Landymore, F. (2025, March 15). Study finds that AI search engines are wrong an astounding proportion of the time. Yahoo Tech. https://www.yahoo.com/tech/study-finds-ai-search-engines-151517475.html

2 | Haden, J. (2023, January 13). Why Do So Many Prices End in 9? How Left-Digit Bias Increases Sales and Boosts Profits. Inc. https://www.inc.com/jeff-haden/why-do-so-many-prices-end-in-9-how-left-digit-bias-increases-sales-boosts-profits.html

Crawl first, succeed sooner

2

Learning Objectives

By the end of this chapter, readers will be in a position to outline the considerations involved before creating a marketing campaign. They will be capable of articulating the five-subject carousel of posts. Students will be able to classify target markets.

Tech needed to use Create with AI

Depending on the specific AI application, accessing AI technology may require a compatible device, such as a computer, smartphone, or smart home assistant, as well as a stable internet connection. While some features may operate offline with "on-device AI" capabilities, the majority of advanced AI functions necessitate a cloud connection for data processing and access to AI models.

Most AI applications require a reliable internet connection with enough bandwidth, particularly when utilizing cloud-based AI services. A gigabit (1000 mbps) connection is ideal for more demanding AI applications, such as real-time processing or large data sets, where there should be minimal delay or lag time between an input and its corresponding response in a system. This ensures a near-real-time experience by transmitting data with minimal delay. It's essential for applications like online gaming, live video streaming, and high-frequency trading, where quick reactions are required, which is often achieved through a fiber optic connection. However, in order to use AI technology effectively, you usually need a high-speed internet connection with a minimum download speed of 100 Mbps.

Large data transfers are common in AI applications; hence, processing speed depends on a rapid connection. Real-time AI interactions get the best outcomes; that is, when you prompt or modify an AI program, it takes effect as you are editing.

A slower speed might be adequate if you intend to use AI for simple tasks like text generation.

More bandwidth is needed for sophisticated applications like machine learning or video analysis.

The AI program should work well on your device if it has sufficient memory and processing capability. The majority of AI apps work with widely used operating systems like iOS and Android. To access the needed capabilities, such as Google Assistant, Siri, Alexa, or other AI-powered productivity tools, you will need to select a certain AI platform or app.

These days, some gadgets include "on-device AI" capabilities, which enable fundamental AI operations even in the absence of a live internet connection. This technique reduces the need for continuous cloud connectivity by processing data locally on a device, which is particularly advantageous for real-time applications.

Considerations before creating a marketing campaign

Marketing's function is to create, communicate, deliver, and exchange offerings that value customers, clients, partners, and society at large, essentially aiming to attract and retain customers by understanding their needs and developing strategies to reach them, ultimately driving business growth through sales and brand awareness.

Marketers are responsible for overseeing all the components of a campaign. The materials should attract and retain customers by understanding their needs and developing strategies to meet them, driving business growth through sales and brand awareness. They oversee campaign components by first gathering customer and competitor information to understand market trends. This involves conducting research, analyzing data, and staying updated with industry movements to identify opportunities and threats.

IMAGE 2-1

Social media post need to grab the reader's attention and supply information that interests them.

AI Practicum | Prompt on Creator: Man holding an iPhone, reading a social post, falling asleep.

They also focus on designing products or services that meet expectations. This means collaborating with product development teams to ensure offerings align with consumer desires and stand out in the marketplace.

Setting the optimal price point is another crucial task. Marketers analyze cost structures, competitor pricing, and perceived value to determine a pricing strategy that maximizes profit while remaining attractive to customers.

Communicating value through advertising and public relations, including social media, is key. Effective marketing messages are crafted and disseminated across various channels to build brand awareness and persuade potential customers of the value of the products or services.

As a marketing designer, you need to know limitations and goals. There are terms such as K.I.S.S. and S.M.A.R.T. that are integral to marketing. K.I.S.S. applies to the message itself and stands for Keep it simple, stupid. But to clarify the "simple" part, think "short." Follow K.I.S.S. and develop an attention-grabbing headline. The shorter your message, the better chance it will be read and remembered.

S.M.A.R.T. is an acronym to plan, schedule, and design a campaign that helps marketers set an agenda for a social media campaign. Perhaps the most overlooked part of a strategy is measuring a campaign's success. When starting to develop the posts and a schedule, make sure there is a clear goal that can be validated. Examples are reposting, comments, and likes, but the best is a response to your call to action.

People have all kinds of ideas about the fundamentals of visual marketing. However, that list should include what marketing is not. It does not create a need for a product. Marketing can inform people what product they need or seem to want. Marketing's function is to help drive sales, but if the product has no intrinsic value to potential customers, it will not sell. For example, your company may have the best roof to repel hail, but if the area it is being sold into only has damaging hail every five years, it is doubtful that company will be successful.

The customer and their needs and desires are the main focus of the most effective sales and marketing communications. This entails tailoring the message to each individual.

Download options with Creator

Reformat options with Creator

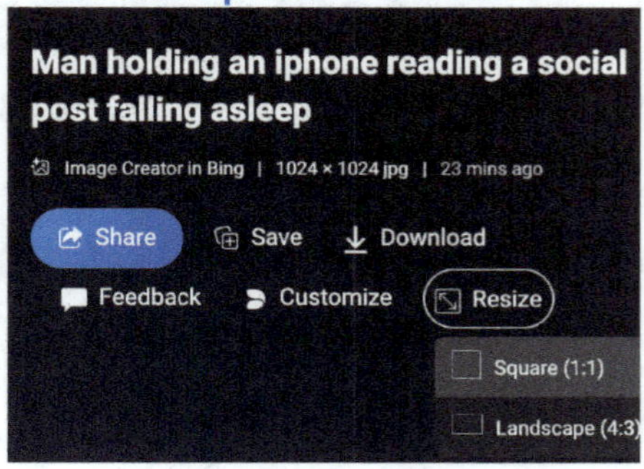

IMAGE 2-2

Options in Creator to scale the image in two different views: portrait and landscape. Note other image AI generators have more options, such as TV screen landscape width.

Key points about sales literature:

Marketing's function is to increase customer engagement with a company.

The Why: To promote a product or service and generate leads or sales.

The Who: Potential target customers or existing clients.

The How: A marketing communication that includes information about the product or service and how it benefits the reader.

The What: A call to action, which can be a compelling offer or a direction to follow.

The When: A time period or an expiration date that is not too far off, or the reader will put it off to be done later.

The Where: An address, website (a QR code along with the address), or phone number to go to for the product or service.

IMAGE 2-3

Note that AI generators have difficulty with not enough fingers (see 2-1 Image), too many hands, feet, or, in this case, the man has too many arms. I warned my daughter when she went to college about guys like this.

Preparation will save time

Before you start to create marketing such as a social post, a printed flyer, a prospecting email, an outreach text, or various marketing promotions, write or use AI to write the headline and paragraph content if needed. Here is a list of some items you should consider:

Define the goal: What the post is about.

Company logo: It will need to be in a JPG or PNG file and the approximate size and color source. RGB for screen images and CMYK for printing.

Details list such as offers, deadlines, benefits, or key info.

Decide on the call to action: What do you want people to do?

Be prepared to choose colors. Keep consistency with your brand's colors.

High-Quality Images: Product images, background visuals, or illustrations.

Hashtags: These help reach more people across platforms.

Blogging

When Google first became a powerful search engine in the early 2000s, posting articles and personal opinions was already a popular way to spread information. Google worked their algorithm for search results to include blogs. A blog is a website updated regularly that offers insights on specific topics. The term "blog" combines "web" and "log." Originally, blogs were online diaries for daily life logs. Then black hat SEO discovered that if they stuffed the blog with keywords, they were ranked high in search results.

Google in 2011 and later updates greatly reduced keyword stuffing's effectiveness. And in fact, penalized major companies for keyword stuffing, and many of these companies have switched their freelance writers. Many writers have reported a loss of 90% of their blog traffic from Google. Recently, HubSpot, which provides a built-in blogging tool within its CRM platform, lost 80% of its blog traffic.

Having relevant content on your site can bring in more customers than social posts.

It is important to know the difference between the information. Content is considered an article if it meets certain criteria, such as having a structured format and focusing on factual content. If an informational blog has no followers or readers, it is really an article. While blogs can help with search results, current in-depth articles without personal opinion rank better—unless it is a well-known author. Google SGE appears to like human-written, up-to-date information.

A website that focuses on content, such as news and government sites mainly providing information through text, images, and occasionally videos, has a better chance of showing up higher in search results than a personal blog without any traffic. Typically, information websites lack functionalities like comment accounts or forums. Websites providing company product details, blogs about hobbies, or other content do not receive much traffic based on search results.

Blogs and articles should provide knowledge, opinions, or advice. Typically, the written content should display in reverse chronological order, with the latest post first. They should be frequently updated. The content is organized by tags, making it easy to navigate. Additionally, it is often shared on social media platforms. Both blogs and articles serve as creative and marketing tools.

Searchers are looking for information, and Google provides results. Google's AI search results will give an overview and list sources near or at the top of the page. In your marketing schedule, publish articles that are about your industry and interest potential customers.

Specs: Articles

	Voice	Words	Need by
MGDwAI	Expand	500 - 750	2/28/25
HDG-web	Creative	500 - 751	3/1/25
I&I- mag	Friendly	500 - 752	3/2/25
Learn AI	Expert	500 - 753	2/28

IMAGE 2-4

Example of article publication specifications and type of narrative to keep a consistent voice.

Practicum: Use Apple Numbers, Google Sheets, or Microsoft Excel to create easy-to-follow directions.

Target markets

Defined by shared characteristics such as demographics, interests, and behaviors, a "target market" is a particular group of consumers in the marketing industry. This enables companies to concentrate their marketing initiatives on the most probable purchasers of their products. Marketers determine target markets by examining variables such as age, gender, income, location, lifestyle, and requirements. Companies can optimize their campaigns and messages to resonate with each demographic by segmenting the market as a whole.

If you are posting, creating website articles, and developing printed materials, the AI-powered QuillBot has the ability to paraphrase using a voice you choose. Choose a voice from a variety of options, including Standard, Academic, Formal, or Creative. For example, Facebook should have a different tone than LinkedIn. It can rephrase sentences and paragraphs while maintaining the original meaning, making it useful for avoiding plagiarism or simply rewording parts of your text for better clarity. By providing different rephrasing options, QuillBot can help you refine your writing and find the best way to express your ideas to your audience.

√ Use AI to test and create effective headlines

√ Match voice to target market

√ Incorporate the brand's elements subtly

√ Include a CTA (Call to Action)

√ Use hashtags and emojis sparingly

√ Post at peak engagement times

√ Use analytics to track performance

NEETS: The five content pillars of posts

Newsworthy: It should inform followers about your business, your industry, and your team. Example: As a contractor, post before and after images, but make sure it is obviously better. Time-lapse photography is a good presentation tool.

Entertaining: Always high up in views if presented correctly. Make sure whatever you are sharing is positive for the company and brands the company. It does not need to be humorous. It can include behind-the-scenes information or an unusual story.

Emotional: This type of post needs to be share-worthy. It needs to be impactful and relatable. Show the company's involvement with the community. Include employee-focused stories. Example: If you are a family-owned company, show all the generations involved but do not give out names or personal information except for the business principles.

Testimonials: When a job is finished and the quality control team member is going over it with a customer, ask the customer if they are satisfied. If they are, ask if you could film a 30-second video to post of their thoughts. Only use first names and general locations. Make sure they include what was done and why your company exceeded expectations. Have a written permission slip for them to sign—but keep it short. If you use ChatGPT to write it, make sure you proofread and edit the language to be much shorter. About 90% of consumers trust video testimonials.

Specials: If you are having a promotion, explain it with the important details and an expiration date. The deal needs to encourage viewers to use your company, so make sure they understand why they need the offer.

The word *SALE* has a significantly lower engagement than using the term *OFF* with regards to a discounted on the price.

Content focus for your posts

Experts have a number of opinions on the quantity of each subject category for a social media campaign. The 80/20 rule is popular, where 80% of your content should be valuable to your audience and 20% should be promotional. With all the posts competing for attention, if you only focus 20% on your company information, it may be missed.

The 1/3 rule seems more practical since the content is divided into thirds. One-third promotes your brand or product, one-third shares relevant industry news or insights, and one-third engages with your audience through conversation and interaction.

As a marketer or small business owner, your time is precious. Do not waste your time posting because you think it will improve your branding. If the posts do not catch a potential customer's attention, your brand will not be remembered. You want to get your brand out there, where they store that one service by your company so they can retrieve it when it comes up.

The best way for them is to go to the social platform and scroll down, looking for something about your company they remember. If the goal of your post is for viewers to remember your brand, have the same template look with all of your posts. You may have an unusual border with your company logo included, or you always have shadows behind your images, or they always have a bright green background.

For the customer to find you this way, that means you need to post repeatedly. The customer will be able to scroll and find your post with your contact information.

Ingredients for a memorable post

When developing a strong social post, consider the length of the content, the attention grabber, the hook, and the best time to publish it. Sounds basic but in the over-populated world of posts, these are not easily created.

1 Cup of Engagement

Comments, shares, and clicks significantly increase a post's visibility. When crafting a social media post, focus on boosting engagement. Use clear and simple language, coupled with a cooperative tone. To further enhance engagement, employ hashtags related to trending topics. Additionally, consider offering special promotions, contests, and giveaways. Companies should recognize that social networks operate as dual-channel mediums, facilitating both conversations and audience interactions.

2-5 IMAGE

Image illustrating the options for a post where subjects are mixed together. Too many messages, and they are too difficult to read.

AI Practicum | Canva prompt: show a clear mixing bowl with the words action, entertaining, update, offers, news, BOGO, and marketing being mixed in with a spoon.

2 Cups of Visuals

Social media platforms have evolved substantially since their inception.

Although text-based content remains effective in B2B marketing, posts incorporating visuals, such as innovative graphics, images of people, and short-form videos, possess a distinct advantage. Engaging and high-quality visuals, including photos, GIFs, or videos that reflect your company's ethos, pique audience interest. Visual content tends to receive more shares, comments, and clicks compared to purely text-based posts.

3 Tablespoons of High-Quality Content

Generate thoughtful and creative content that enhances brand lead generation, strengthens engagement, and promotes customer retention. Keep messages concise and focused on a single goal and match the voice to the target market. If necessary, create additional posts to convey separate messages.

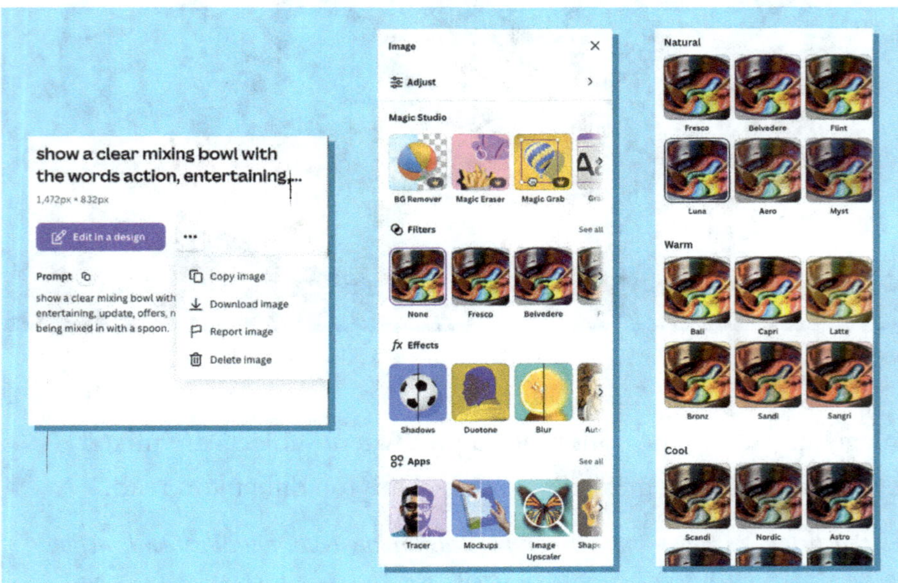

IMAGE 2-6

Options to edit the image in Canva.

AI Practicum | When selecting download, the 'edit in design' button will be available.

Stir and Serve For Best Flavor: Post at peak engagement times. Assess the frequency and timing of your posts. Experiment with different times of day and posting frequencies to determine optimal engagement levels.

- Facebook 9am-10am on weekdays
- YouTube Best: 2pm - 4pm, on weekdays Next: 9am - 11am, on weekends
- Instagram Best: 7am - 8am on weekdays
- LinkedIn Best: 9am - 5pm on weekdays
- Snapchat Best: 10pm and 1am

Analytics suggest that posting during the times listed above is generally the most effective. However, platform-specific recommendations indicate that your target market's availability also comes into play. Facebook posts perform well on Saturdays between 12-3 PM and 6-9 PM since it is the weekend. Instagram posts shown above are best based on the age market and their availability. However, posts are nearly as successful from 10 AM to 2 PM on Tuesdays and Wednesdays.

Try other times and measure engagement. Each social media platform has a specific following. Not only should the strategy reflect those traits, but the creative should also be focused on the recipients.

Social media content tools

3

Learning Objectives

The learner will be qualified to simulate what makes viewers look at marketing. They will be competent to describe the message. The user will be prepared to select the proper typography for a project.

IMAGE 3-1

AI Practicum | Prompt Google Gemini: Create an image of AI robot as an AI assistant for writing

Creating and improving written content with AI

Many AI content generators are available, and each has their own positives and negatives. Some AI apps are actually more like AI editors that can paraphrase and proof existing content that should be used in workflows since most of the AI content generators make grammar and spelling mistakes.

Maintaining an engaging social media presence is challenging, but AI-powered apps can help create captivating content. Here are some of the best AI apps to elevate your social media game.

QuillBot should be considered an AI writing assistant. Its primary function is a paraphrasing tool, meaning it can't generate entirely new content from scratch; instead, it rewrites existing text you provide, allowing you to modify and improve upon it to create your own content, rather than directly creating content for you like some other AI writing tools. Pricing: Free version and paid Pro version.

Grammarly spots plagiarism and shows the probability of your text being flagged as AI-generated and underlines the flagged text. The AI detector shows the percentage of text that appears AI-generated and offers guidance on interpreting the results responsibly. Grammarly is useful for improving writing with its grammar, spelling, and style suggestions. The tone detector ensures your brand's voice resonates with your target market. It also provides engagement insights to refine your content strategy. Make sure you proof the content since Grammarly has had problems with confusing the word spelling and choices with the U.S., U.K., and other English-speaking countries. Pricing: Free version and paid Pro versions.

ChatGPT is one of the most well-known and more versatile content generators due to its user-friendly interface and ability to produce diverse content types. It is amazing what it can do, such as writing a Valentine's Day poem for your spouse or creating the content for games such as Murder Mysteries. Pricing: Free version and paid Pro versions.

Microsoft Word can create content rewrites and drafts as you write within the app. You ask a question or describe the topic to write. Not a very well-known feature is the free version offered on the internet. Pricing: Free version and paid personal and business versions.

Google Gemini Writing, a feature in Google Docs, is a strong source for content creation and, as an AI assistant for writing, brainstorming, summarizing, and drafting posts, emails, and marketing literature. Pricing: Users 18 and older with a Google account and educators with a school account can use Gemini for free.

IMAGE 3-2

Image created with Photoshop.

Guidelines for creating successful social posts

K.I.S.S. for marketing is basically keeping your post to one message and one goal. Short is a better solution and not as likely to be passed over. Shorter posts around 80 characters are more engaging, and as a rule of thumb, collect more likes, comments, and shares.[1]

For a social media post, experts such as BuzzSumo, a marketing company for content creation, researched what constitutes a "good" headline. They analyzed more than 100 million posts on Facebook and Twitter (it was not X yet). The results found that the most engagement received by headlines had less than 65 characters and 11 words.[2]

To keep your posts' content short, you can add links to landing pages. Keep them short, 13 words or less, because the link description will be ignored by a number of readers if it is too long.

Hootsuite's research found that on paid posts, for the best engagement, messages should be limited to under 19 words to be read. Every Facebook ad needs three types of content: a headline, ad text, and a link description. They discovered that people only read the first 5 words of a headline. In the text above the ad, people stopped reading after 19 words.[3]

Compared to purchasing two and receiving a third for half price, using the term BOGO yields better returns.

A significant portion of people stop reading a message when a post's content stops with ellipses trying to get the reader to click and read more. They don't click to continue reading. Properly presented offers attract attention.

The structure of a well-designed post

Begin by drafting an outline of your post and gradually refine it by removing unnecessary words until you achieve a concise version. Research has indicated that people tend to scan online content rather than read it word for word. Use AI tools to generate content ideas based on those phrases. Be careful not to let the verbiage sound too robotic and flat. Check and do not stray from your established social media goals, such as brand awareness, lead generation, and sales. Track your social media analytics to see what works best for your business and refine your strategy. Consider your target audience and their preferred platforms and posting times.

Humor

You will discover that what is amusing to you is not to someone else—it is subjective. However, with the aid of AI, you can create cartoon images to help visualize the funny story. Irreverent humor is the easiest but also the most dangerous since it can easily offend someone. Your viewer may overlook dry humor as they skim the posts. At first, you may want to use wordplay with the image until you know your audience.

Images

Showing only a body part or part of a device can be effective since it leaves the rest to the viewer. Playful, lively, bright images get more attention than dark and busy visuals.

User-generated content

Reposting what others have posted is popular because it is simple and leaves the struggle to find something interesting. When posts contain original content, this higher level of effort can lead to a more thorough reading experience for the audience.

Publishing

A company should aim to post on social media platforms a few times per week, with specific frequencies varying by platform. Have a checklist of different content types. Rotate the focus between images, content, contests, games, cartoons, work products, and videos to engage with your audience.

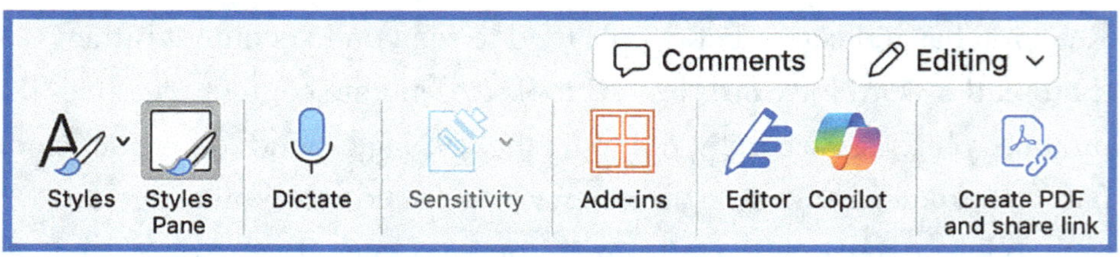

IMAGE 3-3

Screen grab of Copilot app location on the toolbar on Home tab.

How to use Copilot

To use Copilot in Microsoft Word, start by opening a Word document. Next, select the text, list, or table that you want to work with and click the Copilot icon in the left margin or in the toolbar next to Editor. Once you have done this, choose the "Make changes" option. In the "Draft with Copilot" dialog that appears, specify your request. You can then select "Keep it," "Regenerate," or "Discard it."

Additionally, you can use the "Inspire me" button to generate content. For better responses, make sure to provide detailed information in Copilot's compose box. There are several options available: you can choose "Rewrite" to revise the text, select "Visualize as a table" to format the text as a table, click "Adjust tone" to change the tone of the text, or choose "Regenerate" for new responses.

IMAGE 3-4

Humor is in the eye of the beholder.

AI Practicum | Prompt Microsoft Creator: Illustrate a 3D thumbs up with bright colors and confetti.

You can use Word to generate most of a social media post with Copilot, but you'll need to personalize it for your audience and platform. To use

Copilot for a social post, give a clear prompt. In the Copilot chat box, provide details like topic and tone, such as informative and promotional or humorous. You can include the target audience, and desired length.

Afterward, review and edit the draft post generated by Copilot to ensure it matches your brand voice, includes relevant hashtags, and suits the platform. Customization is key: adjust wording and tone to fit your brand and audience. Consider visuals: add images or graphics separately, as Copilot can't generate these. Check for accuracy: double-check facts and details, especially when promoting products or services.

Copilot Standard Post

To create a straightforward post with the prompt: Write a Facebook post announcing a new flooring. Highlight key features and include a call-to-action to visit our website. After the post was created, it was changed to call for an appointment and to add an expiration date to the offer. The following content was the AI results:

Introducing Our New Flooring Collection!

We are thrilled to announce the launch of our latest flooring collection, designed to elevate the beauty and functionality of your home. Here are some of the key features:

√ **Durability**: Our flooring is built to withstand heavy foot traffic and everyday wear and tear.

√ **Stylish Designs**: Choose from a wide range of modern and classic designs to match your decor.

√ **Easy Maintenance**: Enjoy hassle-free cleaning and maintenance with our innovative flooring solutions.

√ **Eco-Friendly**: Made from sustainable materials, our flooring is environmentally friendly and safe for your family.

√ **Special Offer**: Get an exclusive **20% discount** on your first purchase! Use code **FLOOR20** when you call to schedule a no-obligation appointment. Offer expires (Insert Date)

Don't miss out on transforming your space with our stunning new flooring options! Visit our website now to explore the full collection and find the perfect fit for your home.

(Insert Telephone Number)

Visit Our Website: (Insert website URL)

#NewFlooring #HomeImprovement #EcoFriendly #StylishDesigns #DurableFlooring #EasyMaintenance #SpecialOffer

Copilot Humorous Post:

Write a humorous post about a grand opening sale for a vapor store with a target market of 25-35-year-olds. Include a CTA to come by and receive a Free gummy. AI Results:

Grand Opening Alert!

Hey there, vape enthusiasts! We're beyond excited to announce the grand opening of our brand-new vapor store, and we've got some smokin' deals just for you!

Why You Should Swing By:

- **Epic Discounts**: Get ready to save big on all your favorite vape gear and e-liquids.
- **Cool Vibes**: Our store is decked out with the latest and greatest in vape tech. It's like a candy store for adults!
- **Free Gummies**: Yes, you read that right! Come by and receive a FREE gummy with every purchase. Because who doesn't love free stuff?

So, what are you waiting for? Grab your friends, head on over, and let's make some clouds together!

Visit Us Today! (Insert location address and telephone number.)

#GrandOpening #VapeLife #EpicDeals #FreeGummies #VapeStore

Three different image generators with the same prompt.

IMAGE 3-5

AI Practicum | Prompt Adobe Express: Create a 3D image of the word Headline as tall as the clouds. Note the misspelling of the word headline.

IMAGE 3-6

AI Practicum | Prompt Google Gemini: Create a 3D image of the word Headline as tall as the clouds.

IMAGE 3-5C

Humor is in the eye of the beholder.

AI Practicum | Prompt Microsoft Creator: Create a 3D image of the word Headline as tall as the clouds. Note the misspelling of the word headline.

Do not rely on AI tools to be accurate and produce easy to read content. Review and edit the generated text to ensure it aligns with your brand voice and is accurate for your audience. Essentially, use ChatGPT as a starting point and then customize it to fit your needs. ChatGPT 3.5 is the free version, and ChatGPT 4.0 is a subscription that is higher than many other large language AI models.

How to use ChatGPT 3.5 for social posts

Sign into OpenAI ChatGPT and paste a clear prompt from your list of options written earlier. Define the specific details about your post, including the topic, target audience, desired tone (funny, informative, inspirational), and platform you're posting on.

An interesting creative concept with ChatGPT is its ability to generate variations if you ask for them. You can use ChatGPT for brainstorming ideas and get creative feedback for post topics and points of view. The ideas allow you to easily add your own unique perspective.

Two benefits of using ChatGPT for social media posts are the ability to generate a basic post structure with copy in seconds and overcome creative writing roadblocks. Make sure there are not too many relevant hashtags, and finish with a brilliant call to action.

On the final ready-to-go-to-publish post, question it to make sure it is the best message, it represents the company's style, and it has the correct narrative to engage your audience.

The most important consideration on a social post is engagement. Do not rely solely on ChatGPT for engaging content. There are many news stories about people who did not proof the content.

ChatGPT 3.5 Standard Post:

Create a straightforward post with the prompt: Write a Facebook post announcing a new flooring. Highlight key features and include a call-to-action to visit our website. In place of the √, GPT had 3D check emojis, and a number of distracting emojis were spread throughout. AI Results:

Exciting News! Upgrade Your Space with Our New Flooring.

We're thrilled to introduce our latest premium flooring options—designed for style, durability, and comfort! Whether you're refreshing your home or upgrading your business, our new collection offers:

√ Elegant & Modern Designs to match any décor
√ Durable & Easy to Maintain for long-lasting beauty
√ Comfort & Quality you can feel with every step

Transform your space today! Visit our website to explore the collection: [Insert Website Link]

#NewFloors #HomeUpgrade #StylishLiving

ChatGPT Humorous Post:

Prompt to ChatGPT: Write a humorous post about a grand opening sale for a vapor store with a target market of 25-35-year-olds. Include a CTA to come by and receive a Free gummy.

Note that instead of Xs, GPT had a map location pin; instead of a Y, GPT had a calendar icon. In place of the √, there were flame cones. A number of distracting emojis, such as rockets, smiley faces, clouds, were spread throughout. Perhaps GPT assumes 25-35-year-olds like emojis. ChatGPT 3.5 AI Results:

Grand Opening Sale—Come Vape & Chill!

Big news, folks! Our brand-new vapor store is OPEN, and we're kicking things off with a grand opening sale that's smoother than your favorite flavor!

What's in it for you?
√ Huge discounts on top-tier vapes & juices
√ A chill vibe with zero judgment (we see you, cloud chasers)
√ FREE gummy just for stopping by! (Because who doesn't love free stuff?)

So, grab your crew and come celebrate with us! Your taste buds will thank you. Pull up, puff up, and pick up your free gummy!

X [Insert Store Location]
Y [Insert Date]

#VapeLife #GrandOpening #PuffPuffPassBy #FreeGummies

Strong responses use strong AI practices

To write an engaging headline, keep it concise, use strong action verbs, include specific details or numbers, address your audience's interests, ask questions to pique curiosity, ensure clarity about the topic, and be relevant to your content. Two recommendations that always work are to create a sense of urgency that leads to the CTA and use words that have an emotional impact or reaction.

The structure of headlines has been studied for engagement since the 1960s. Headlines with about 6 words get more clicks. However, I have found 5 or 7 words have more responses. Using adjectives and action words makes them more interesting.

Some statistics can be debated, and tests have shown both sides to be correct. Examples where the stats can be used for either argument for or against a rule:

$ Positive or negative sentiment is better than neutral phrases.

$ Use of common and uncommon words is always debated depending on your analyzer.

$ Headlines with numbers are better at engagement.

AI is a very good tool for creating posts and marketing headlines, as well as some AI tools that can analyze your headline. There are a number of options, but some are more to pull you in and get you to pay.

Easy-Peasy AI headline generator, powered by GPT-4, is an AI-powered tool that helps in creating catchy, relevant, and engaging titles for articles, blog posts, YouTube titles, landing pages, newspapers, SEO, and more. It uses information such as the topic and the tone you want for your title to generate various headline suggestions.

You can have a free account with over 200 headline templates. Fill out the topic and the tone, such as catchy, energetic, or clever. If you try to enable "'Use advanced AI model," it will give you a choice in price plans. For the free version, select Generate and see what you think. What they don't tell you is that you only get 2 free headlines a day. 20 average headlines were generated.

Prompted Easy-Peasy to write a Facebook headline announcing a new flooring.

Under the category of Guides & How-To

How to Choose the Perfect Flooring for Your Home: A Step-by-Step Guide

The Ultimate Guide to Installing Your New Flooring Like a Pro

(Plus 3 more options)

Under the category of Questions

What Flooring Options Will Elevate Your Home's Style This Season?

Are You Ready to Upgrade Your Floors? Here's What You Need to Know!

(Plus 3 more options)

Under the category of listicles

10 Stunning Flooring Options to Transform Your Home Instantly

7 Reasons Why You Should Invest in New Flooring Today

5 Flooring Trends You Can't Miss in 2023

8 Benefits of Upgrading Your Flooring That Will Surprise You

(Plus 6 more options)

If ChatGPT, had been prompted, there would be one result, "New Floors, New Look! Upgrade Your Space Today!"

EXPERIMENT WITH PROMPTS

The following are three appraisals of two different results from Adobe Firefly. The prompts had identical wording, except for one word—cartoon and photographic. The subject is the same, but the visual is different.

IMAGE 3-8A

AI Practicum | Firefly Prompt: Create a cartoon image for an ad announcing a new flooring with a content area with eerie lighting and confetti that comes from the window.

IMAGE 3-8A

AI Practicum | Firefly Prompt: Create a photographic image for an ad announcing a new flooring with a content area with eerie lighting and confetti that comes from the window.

SEO Review Tools has a free headline writer. It is free and asks what keywords you are using. It had 25 very energetic and different results, but the top three were:

"Transform Your Space with Our Stunning Selection of Flooring"

"Revamp Your Decor with Our Latest Flooring Trends"

"Find Your Perfect Match: Browse Our New Flooring Options

Headline analyzers using AI tools

The free AI analyzers make you go through the 'prove you are human verification' and then take about two minutes to give you a score; Sharethrough will even give you better options.

Overall, it may not be worth the time it takes for the free options but try them out before subscribing.

When the headline "Revamp Your Decor with Our Latest Flooring Trends" was analyzed, Sharethrough called it average, and its top suggestion was "Transform Your Living Space with Trending Flooring Options," which is interesting if you look at the previous AI-generated list.

When IsItap was used to analyze "Transform Your Living Space with Trending Flooring" options, it gave it an average score and noted it had too many words.

AI robots and AI assistants are playing an increasingly important role in writing. They serve as useful tools for various types of writers, enhancing productivity, accuracy, and creativity.

Disclaimer

When using generative AI tools for creating images and designs, the results are generally available for commercial purposes. According to the US Copyright Office (see below), copyright ownership cannot be claimed for any of the images. AI-generated images may infringe on third-party intellectual property rights. Please review the "Generative AI Terms of Use" for any AI tools you utilize.

The US Copyright Office has confirmed that AI-generated material and suggestions are not protected by copyright. In its report, *Copyright and Artificial Intelligence, Part 2: Copyrightability*, the office concluded that "Copyright protects the original expression in a work created by a human author, even if the work also includes AI-generated material." Conversely, copyright does not apply to AI-generated content that includes some human content. The report clarified that from a graphic design standpoint, artificial intelligence is copyrightable if it is used as a tool to style or produce effects in human-generated work. For definitive guidance on your design, consult a copyright attorney. The report is available at: copyright.gov/ai/Copyright-and-Artificial-Intelligence-Part-2-Copyrightability-Report.pdf

1 | Bullas, J. (2024, August 20). 10 Powerful Tips to Increase Fan Engagement on Facebook. Jef's Jabs. https://www.jeffbullas.com/10-powerful-tips-to-increase-fan-engagement-on-facebook

2 | Linehan, L., Rayson, S., & Chiu, H. W. (2023, November 4). 100m Articles analyzed: What you need to write the best headlines. BuzzSumo.com. https://buzzsumo.com/blog/most-shared-headlines-study/#section-4

3 | McLachlan, S. (2025, January 2). Ideal length of social media posts A guide for every platform. Social Media Marketing & Management Dashboard. https://blog.hootsuite.com/ideal-social-media-post-length

Image tools for creating social posts

4

Learning Objectives.

The learner will be in a position to discuss a number of AI apps to create images. They will know how to draw attention with a strong visual image and will illustrate the uses of each marketing design file type.

IMAGE 4-1

AI practicum | Craiyon prompt: Close-up of a person looking at the viewer; Aspect ratio 16x9.

Visuals draw attention

Research indicates that video posts generate far higher engagement than text-only posts. The human brain processes visual information significantly more rapidly than textual information. Audiences are more inclined to remember information presented in a video. Posts with visual content, specifically pictures, get triple the engagement of text posts. Carousel posts are more engaging than single photos. Photos with human faces get more likes than photos without faces.

When creating pictures, use lighter images with more background and less close-up. individuals do not like to have peopleright in their face. Use bluish or cool-toned images instead of reddish, yellowish, or warm images. Cool colors are calming, more popular, and usually do not conflict with brand colors. Reds and yellows are action colors that are good for CTAs but can cause people to feel waned or uncomfortable. Interior designers know that bedrooms should be painted with calming cool colors and entertainment rooms with bright and active warm colors. Do not boost the saturation levels of colors in images. It is obvious the image has been manipulated for attention. It can cause the viewer to doubt the realism of the image.

IMAGE 4-2

Showing more of the person's face allows the viewer to sense an emotion and react.

AI practicum | Craiyon prompt: Show a person looking at the viewer; aspect ratio 4x3.

Image resolution is critical.

Images utilized in printing possess a resolution of 300 dots per inch, which is four times greater than the 72 pixels per inch (ppi) of screen images. Numerous screens display images at 100 pixels per inch (ppi).

Posts and internet marketing materials should be produced at a resolution of 100 ppi or higher. You can reduce resolution at any time but raising it more than 20% will result in a dull and unfocused image. Indeed, commencing with a higher-resolution image and subsequently reducing it can enhance the perceived sharpness of the image.

When working on a print image, most digital artists work in the RGB mode and then convert to CMYK. Photoshop has most of the filters and effects set for RGB. For web images, start in red, green, and blue mode and keep it there. If you convert from printing colors to digital screen colors, the hues will be less saturated, have less contrast, and be duller.

With advancements in technology for higher-resolution monitors, color palettes have been enhanced. They exhibit greater dynamism and complexity. Utilize color to captivate viewers but be mindful that monitors do not consistently exhibit the same colors, tones, saturation, and sharpness.

Marketing design file types.

In addition to the software editable file formats such as PSD, INDD, and DOC labels, visual designers use a number of types of image files for website and print design. The final result decides which one is appropriate for the final mechanical.

File format: TIFF

In fields where high-resolution images are essential, such as photography, art printing, graphic design, and publishing, this pixel-based format is frequently utilized. When compressing a TIFF (Tagged Image File Format) file, the picture quality remains the same. Although these features are fantastic for preservation and high-end printing, they produce files that are too big to be used on the web. TIFF files are ideal for photos requiring a wide spectrum of colors and tones since they can have a very high color depth, such as 16-bit or 32-bit. Transparency, numerous layers, and metadata storage (including color profiles) are all features of TIFF files that are similar to Photoshop.

File format: GIF

You can save still pictures and animated images in a GIF file. According to Stephen Wilhite, the creator of the Graphics Interchange Format (GIF), the "g" in GIF is pronounced similarly to the word "general." By integrating numerous frames into a single file, this format may accommodate basic animations. Short, repeated animations, buttons, and banners are among the most common uses for GIFs on the web. The general public uses GIFs—short video clips—for memes, social networking, and communications purposes.

Due to their 8-bit color palette and 256 colors, GIFs are unable to display sophisticated, high-quality images like photographs, which is a trade-off for keeping file sizes small for the internet. Simple graphics like logos, icons, or illustrations with few colors work well in this format. One-bit transparency is possible in GIFs, meaning that each pixel can be completely opaque or transparent. Unlike other formats, this one does not support gradations.

File format: JPG

This file format minimizes data transfer while preserving the majority of the original image quality. JPG files, which stand for "Joint Photographic Experts Group," reduce file sizes by removing unnecessary details from images. Files are compressed to reduce space; however, image quality may suffer if the file is overly compressed or altered many times. Images with smooth color gradients or pictures do well in this format. Due to its optimal quality-to-file-size ratio, it finds extensive application with digital cameras and web photos.

A transparent backdrop cannot be used with a JPG. It is made for full-color pictures with a white background but a fuzzy white area. With JPG, you may choose from a variety of compression levels to suit your image quality needs. Lower compression preserves quality but produces larger files, while higher compression reduces file size while increasing picture quality.

File format: PNG

An open-source replacement for the GIF format, the Portable Network Graphics (PNG) file was developed. Websites and social media platforms frequently utilize PNG files for picture content due to their ability to compress image data while maintaining original information. When it comes to web design, these files capability for transparent backgrounds is invaluable. When working with various backdrops in web design, this comes in handy for inserting graphics. PNG files are great for complicated images like photos or intricate graphics since they can display millions of colors. You can't use CMYK or animation files in this format.

File format: EPS

Since EPS files may be resized without affecting the image quality, they find widespread application in professional graphic design for logos and drawings. Multiple vector graphic programs are compatible with EPS (Encapsulated PostScript) files, which store vector drawings as mathematical equations. Professional designers and printers choose EPS files when making scalable logos, drawings, and other designs that require precise printing at different sizes without sacrificing quality.

Using AI apps to create images.

The sites that create the best visuals are not necessarily the best sources for designing the posts. You should set up your workflow to write the content in one app, create images in another app, and design the final post in a different app.

Adobe Firefly generates vibrant images that closely align with the prompts, serving as a creative and practical image generation tool. The free version is a trial edition, and there are several premium editions.

Bing **Creator** is a strong image creator and straightforward. Input your description, and it generates your image. For the best results, provide detailed prompts and experiment with different variations to fine-tune your images. Creator can work on other browsers, but to fully utilize the features, it works best on Microsoft Edge. Pricing includes a paid version, or you can use it through your Microsoft Suite subscription.

A vast number of online AI picture generators exist, featuring a diverse array of subscription costs. Try them out before you choose which option is most suitable for you. Additional options to examine include Leonardo AI, Dall-E AI, Fotor, and Freepik's AI image creator.

Before using the generators, compose a detailed depiction of the image to be developed so you can copy and paste it into the prompt field. Add alternate adjectives and settings to manipulate the image creations. This will allow you to use different AI generators to create images until you have the one that you think will communicate your message.

IMAGE 4-3

AI Practicum | Creator used prompt: The words TIFF, GIF, JPG, PNG, EPS swirling around each other in a swamp. Output max size is 5.96 inches wide.

DEMONSTRATION MICROSOFT **CREATOR**

Bing Image Creator is accessible on browsers other than Microsoft Edge, such as Chrome and Safari, by visiting "bing.com/create." However, a browser extension may be required to fully utilize its features.

The AI image generator offered by Bing is simple to use. Users need to sign in with a Microsoft account, visit the generator, provide a description, and the generator will create an image. For optimal results, detailed prompts should be provided, and experimenting with different variations is recommended to refine the images.

Connect to Microsoft Designer to add text, image enhancements, and cropping. Layers can be added to save for editing later.

To use Bing Copilot (also known as Microsoft Copilot), it is preferred to use Microsoft Edge due to the features being directly integrated within the sidebar. Nonetheless, Bing Copilot can also be accessed on other browsers like Chrome by utilizing a dedicated extension. This allows users to access the chat feature on any major web browser by visiting the Bing website.

Users receive a new set of credits at the start of each month, and one credit is deducted from the balance for each interaction with Copilot (e.g., drafting a document in Word) or Designer's AI features (e.g., generating an image based on a description). If free credits are exhausted, users can upgrade to Microsoft 365 Personal or Family, or to Copilot Pro, to acquire additional credits.

Prompt A **Prompt B** **Prompt C**

IMAGE 4-4

AI Practicum | Using Firefly, Prompt A used the 'Photo' style, and in Prompt B and Prompt C, used the 'Art' style. Prompt: Show someone looking at a social post and scratching their head in confusion. The output max size for each square image is 6.8 inches wide.

DEMONSTRATION ADOBE **FIREFLY**

Look at Prompt C. A and B are styles that do not stand out and are overused. But if you were to use C, it would stand out. You just need to make sure the image fits your company's brand.

Go to *firefly.adobe.com* and in the hero image, you will see a field to put in content to generate an image. You can also create videos here.

In the image field, type a detailed description of the image you want to create. This is known as your stage one prompt. After this, you will refine our prompt or completely start over if you realize certain terms are being focused on by the AI generator.

The minimum prompt consists of 5 words or more. However, unlike what the experts state, too detailed a prompt will not get you close to what you are looking to create. Therefore, start with 10 to 15 words that you can adjust or allow Firefly to suggest, and add more descriptive words for better results

Prompt D

Prompt E

IMAGE 4-5

AI Practicum | Using Firefly in Prompt D used 'Storm' style reference and 'Vibrant colors.' In Prompt E, added 'Art' and 'Shot from below.' Prompt: Show someone looking at a social post and scratching their head in confusion.

Select the "Generate" button, which will take you to the main creative board with tools on the side. Firefly assumes you want a square image. If that is not the case, change the aspect ratio to vertical or horizontal. Choose either art or a photo and a reference. If you want to see what Firefly will do, just select a style and, on color tone, choose vibrant colors, and you can choose a camera angle "macrophotography."

Click on one, and in the next window, select upscale. Then download.

DEMONSTRATION **CRAIYON**

Navigate to *craiyon.com* and type in the field a description of the image you would like to create. As with the other generators, try to be descriptive. Choose an aspect ratio and a style, and step back; the page is filled with options. If you scroll down, you will see inspirational ideas for you.

As on most AI generators, make sure you count the fingers and eyes. If you use the free image, it may be out of focus when enlarged, and you need to include the attribute.

Prompt A **Prompt B**

IMAGE 4-6

AI Practicum | Using Craiyon the results include a 'Photo' style see A, and art style see B. The prompt: Someone laughing at something they are reading on their iPhone. The output max size for each square image is 3.4 inches wide.

The resolution of the photos is not as good as that of other generators, which is acceptable for projects involving social media and the internet. For printed marketing, the smaller resolution limits the use of the image.

IMAGE 4-7

AI Practicum | Using Craiyon some of the options from the prompt: Someone laughing at something they are reading on their iPhone.

How to use all-in-one AI for social media

5

Learning Objectives.

By the end of this chapter, the student is expected to be qualified to define all-in-one AI-generative apps. They should be capable of providing an overview of the platforms. The reader is going to be capable of characterizing social media AI generative apps in action.

In the following images numbered 5-1, 5-2, and 5-5, the results were from three different AI generators but had the same prompts. These examples show you which AI you may want to use for an image that follows your prompt. You may decide that you like the creativity that AI takes and go with that approach.

IMAGE 5-1
AI Practicum | Deep Dream Generator prompt: the earth surrounded by social media posts; artistic 2 style

Overview of the platforms

Breakdown of the different social platforms.

How a company is perceived is not only based upon their advertising and posts but also on what platforms they post on. Therefore, marketers must know the narrative of each social platform and its market. Each platform may say they appeal to all people, but as a marketer, you should know who you are communicating with in your posts.

For decades, Facebook has been the most popular social media platform. Therefore, Facebook should be included in any marketer's strategy. According to the Statista Research Department, "As of January 2023, 86 percent of marketing specialists stated that they used Facebook as part of their digital campaigns."[1]

Facebook's sister company Instagram has become the most popular option, with LinkedIn close behind. While Facebook and Instagram are personal interactions, LinkedIn is focused on business relationships, which means the posts and advertising have different creative solutions.

YouTube is a social stage and has a strong how-to base of followers. WhatsApp is used for private messaging and group chat capabilities, and TikTok is made up of short-form creative video content that is trend-driven.

Some social media platforms have strong proponents. X is controlled by Elon Musk, and the Trump Media & Technology Group Corporation runs Truth Social. Both of which are considered conservative platforms. BlueSky is considered to be liberal-leaning and supported by Rachael Maddox and many Democratic politicians.

Marketers use demographics to define a target market most likely to be interested in a product or service. They label groups to make it easier to define the narrative for social posts and ads. Baby boomers were born from 1946 to 1964, followed by Generation X, GenZ for short, who were born from 1965 to 1980.

Millennials, born 1981–1996, are considered to be more tech-savvy than other groups and early adopters of technology. Millennials are more likely to use digital sources for information. They remember what life was like before smartphones. The majority of Millennials use social media, and more than half make online purchases.

The GenZ group was born 1997–2012, straddling both centuries. Today's young children are in the GenA demographic and were born from 2010 to the present and do not know how to operate a rotary dial telephone.

Marketers categorize each generation into key consumer demographics and consider their preferences for social media content. The goal is to tailor their marketing strategies to communicate to your customers how your business connects to them.

Facebook demographics have a wide range in ages, education, and income. Generally, over half the users in the U.S. are female; the main age group is in the 25-54-year-old categories.

YouTube is the second most used social media platform and is owned by Google. It is the largest video-sharing platform worldwide. The age group is 18-34-year-olds; over half of the users are male, with the majority of U.S. teenagers using it.

Instagram is the favorite platform of Gen Z. It is more popular with users under 34 years old, and slightly more males use it than females.

Snapchat's main demographic is Gen Z, with about the same percentage of male and female users.

LinkedIn has become the "business networking platform" and is more popular with the male Millennials. More than half of the members have higher education degrees and have an average income of $100,000.

IMAGE 5-2

AI Practicum | DeepAI prompt: the earth surrounded by social media posts; fantasy world style

Steps for Success

Creating a professional social media post requires a blend of good design, engaging content, and a clear message. The internet is filled with opinions, and many are worthy of reading. Here is an overview of what most experts agree is needed for a successful post.

Before you start creating, write down and define your purpose. By determining your goal, such as promoting a product, sharing an announcement, or increasing engagement, and identifying your target audience, you will stay focused.

It may seem obvious but check that you have the correct format and size: Since they vary, you will need to create different files, so name them appropriately.

Use the brand's colors and maintain consistent fonts. Add relevant icons or graphics.

Follow K.I.S.S. and develop an attention-grabbing headline. Use phrases or questions that attract attention, like "Boost Your Sales in 5 Steps!" See Chapter 3 for information on the AI Headline creator. The body copy should be concise and to the point, matching the tone of the brand voice. Include a CTA, such as "Learn More Click Here."

Incorporate the brand's elements by using the logo subtly but legibly. If viewers see the logo first, most of them will move on. Try to get the potential customers interested in your post and then they will see the logo.

Use hashtags and emojis sparingly. Relevant hashtags can increase reach, and emojis can add personality, but too many will be confusing and cause the viewer to move on.

Post at peak engagement times for your audience and use analytics to track performance and improve future posts. Analyze and try other times and approaches to learn how to engage.

Try different approaches to increase engagement and document the results.

Incorporating a poll, fill-in-the-blank questions, or riddles are options to consider. You may choose humor with strong photos to engage the audience. Share an interesting customer story or experience. Show the behind-the-scenes story with photos and short descriptions. Offer prizes in exchange for engagement, reposting, and sharing with friends. Involve your customers in the creation of a new product or service and let them get creative. Validate your core values with images and content posts.

Try out almost all AI-generative apps

For the best verbiage content, use an AI-generative writer app. Likewise, for the most impactful image, use an AI-generative image creator app. For the most control and time-saving social media AI generation, use an all-in-one app, and there are a number to choose from depending on your tech skills.

The first and most obvious option is ChatGPT. As strong as OpenAI's app is at generating information, ChatGPT 3.5 is not a choice at this time for creating the complete social media post.

IMAGE 5-3

AI Practicum | ChatGPT prompt approach #1: Create an ad with the content "Save $99 on servicing the entire HVAC system. Ends March 31. Colors are blue, black, and grey. Use the coupon FB331."

The free and easy AI is ChatGPT, but...

When asked to design a professional Facebook-optimized post, ChatGPT had good questions but did not have the option to upload a company logo. ChatGPT is a good resource to write your copy; you may be tempted to use it to create the entire post. Here is an example of why you should not use ChatGPT for building marketing designs.

Type of post: business promotion (e.g., product launch, service offer), motivational quote, event announcement, sale/discount offer, or personal branding post.

The specific details needed: What's the discount? (e.g., "50% Off," "Buy One Get One Free"); What product/service is on sale? Sale duration? (e.g., "Limited Time Only," "Ends Feb 20"), brand colors, or theme? (If you have specific colors, let me know!); Any specific text or call to action? (e.g., "Shop Now," "Use Code: SAVE20").

The prompt: Save $99 on servicing the entire HVAC system. Ends March 31. Colors are blue, black, and grey. Use the coupon FB331.

From ChatGPT: "Here's your professional social media post for the HVAC service discount! It features your blue, black, and grey color scheme with clear messaging. Let me know if you need any adjustments!"

Followed by: "I'll design a sleek, engaging post and share it here shortly."

IMAGE 5-4
AI Practicum | ChatGPT prompt approach #2: Create an ad with a technician and the content "Save $99 on servicing the entire HVAC system. Ends March 31. Colors are blue, black, and grey. Use the coupon FB331."

Problems with this solution:
The post design is not quite ready to publish. For example, except for the SAVE $99, the type is sketchy and incomplete. Small scribblings are an indication of small, unreadable content. The man is missing fingers (which is a common problem with AI-generated hands) and is extremely busy. The last item of concern was that the image could not be downloaded as a file suitable for posting. GPT suggested taking a screenshot, which means the image would not be the correct size or resolution for posting or printing. However, the verbiage is well written and can be used with other AI generators.

Choose an AI-generative app that is easy to use for you.

There are five really good options at the top of the long list of AI social media post generators.

Adobe Express is arguably graphic designers go-to AI app for generating graphics, creating posts, marketing pieces, and motion graphics. However, its image creation is limited. You have the option to use an existing image from their library or bring one created in Firefly. It was formerly called Sparks but changed in December 2021 to Express. Oddly enough, in a search, Google did not show that unless you asked specifically. In fact, you can go to Adobe pages selling Spark, which confuses the issue. With many customization options and it being free, this cloud-based app lets you create graphics, videos, web pages, and more. It's aimed at mainstream users, not professional graphic designers. It uses templates, text effects, and content variations. You can use prompts with AI to create images. The paid version includes branding tools, online storage, and a version of the Photoshop Express mobile app. Pricing: Adobe Express has one free individual version, one paid individual plan, and one team level of paid access.

Canva is beginner-friendly with templates. It contains "Magic Write"—the" AI-driven content generator. Canva also creates images, videos, and other media. It's used for personal and commercial projects, including social media graphics. Its interface is designed to be easy to use with drag-and-drop functionality. Create custom brand kits that include logos, templates, color palettes, and fonts. Premium templates, more tools, and unlimited storage with team collaboration features are available with the pro version. Its basic interface provides AI-driven suggestions to assist users in creating visuals for posts, articles, and advertisements. The platform offers pre-designed templates tailored for various social media platforms, ensuring that content remains appropriately sized. Details: Canva has one free version and three levels of paid access. Pricing: Free version and paid Pro versions.

Figma is for detailed design work but still beginner-grade design. The options cannot be manipulated very much compared to features on others. It is a cloud-based design tool used for creating graphics, social media posts, websites, apps, and more. It's popular among designers because multiple people can work on the same design at the same time. You can resize elements easily for different social media platforms. Figma is not easy to use unless you use an existing template, or you are a graphic designer that likes a blank page. Create files from scratch, import designs from sketches, or start from templates. Files are great for collaboration, while your drafts are more personal. If you share the drafts, they are view-only. Details: Figma access is for teams: one free team starter version; a plan that has a fee for individuals but is free for students and educators; and two higher levels of paid access. Pricing: Free version and paid Pro versions.

Bing Copilot, also known as Microsoft Copilot, has the feature built-in directly within the sidebar; however, you can also access Bing Copilot on other browsers like Chrome by using a dedicated extension, allowing you to use it on any major web browser by going to the Bing website and accessing the chat feature. Copilot offers more direct features for generating captions, finding relevant hashtags, and tailoring content to specific social media platforms. It can take prompts and generate complete social media posts, including text and even image ideas, tailored to specific platforms like Instagram, X, or Facebook. You can specify the desired tone of your post as casual, informative, or humorous to match your brand voice. Pricing: Paid business versions.

Google Gemini, formerly known as Bard, offers assistance with writing, brainstorming, and learning. It provides summarization and information retrieval from Gmail or Google Drive, and it is capable of image generation. You can utilize text, voice, photos, and camera for assistance. Additionally, Gemini aids in planning with Google Maps and Google Flights, offers support for writing and coding, and helps with design creation. It also performs data analysis, provides time-saving solutions, and creates learning experiences. You can inquire from Gemini, which will respond using pre-existing knowledge or information gathered from other sources. It can handle text, images, audio, and video. Pricing: Paid personal and business versions.

Social media AI generative apps in action.

Most of the software to create posts is online. You will have to have an account with a password, but some are free, and some have monthly or yearly pricing options. Obviously, the free ones have fewer features, and some of the ones that are not free have 30-day trials.

Social media posts creative software is constantly being updated but some of the basic operating functions will be the same depending on what each website offers. The list of available creative options is too long to mention all of them, but here are the main ones marketers on a budget and small businessmen use. There are a number of sites where you can create content, visual elements, and layouts to the correct sizes for the posts.

The following are general steps to using each program that can get you going immediately. There are books on each AI-generative app that can give you detailed instructions and options. Other social media post creators you may want to try are Picsart,

IMAGE 5-5

We have a winner!

AI Practicum | Google Gemini prompt: image of the earth surrounded by social media posts.

USING **EXPRESS**

Adobe Express offers various templates for creating attractive posts. Users can choose free templates and customize them with fonts, colors, and stock images. They can also design from scratch using design tools and themes. AI features include a social caption generator for better engagement, a text-to-music add-on for soundtracks, and Facebook post scheduling. Furthermore, users can create and schedule posts directly on the platform.

Your first step is to write a description of the image to be generated for use later.

Enter a prompt such as the headline "Ingram Publishing Subject Sales Rank #2 In Computers: Design, Graphics & Media" on an image of fireworks, and include the direction to have area for type.

After the post is created, using the text tool, add the CTA: Get a discount at bestdesigner.website.

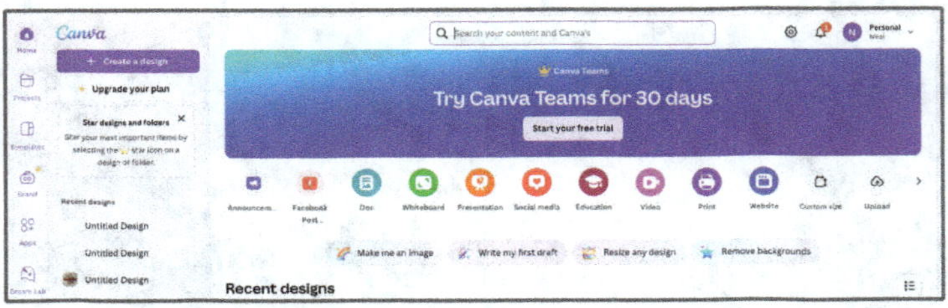

IMAGE 5-6

Canva home page

USING **CANVA**

Canva works well if you use an existing template or import an image. Canva is a good, simple design solution, but if you want to utilize its AI-generated art, it has a ways to go.

It is recommended you write a description of the image to be generated for use later. That way you can drop it in without stopping your creative process. Write or use the Magic Write to create content. From the Home toolbar across the top, select "Social Media" and then choose an option such as "Instagram Post."

At this point, you can choose a template and a style, or in the bottom left of the editor, select Apps. In the "Create something new," select "Imagen" in the bottom left.

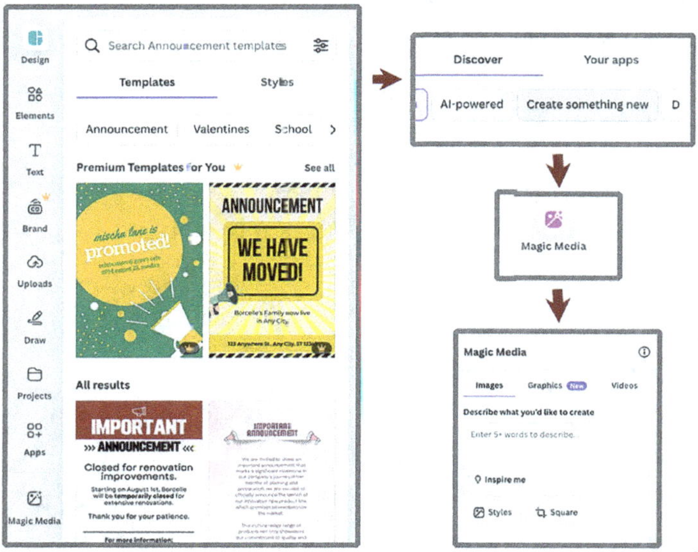

IMAGES 5-7

In the prompt box, paste the description of the image you wrote previously. Select Generate/Create your own. At times when describing the AI image to be generated, the warning that the image violated the policy disclaimer may appear. Back out, refresh, and try again. Select the AI Generator at the bottom labeled Magic Media.

Add text, choose a font, and adjust with the Text Tool bar located at the top. Make sure your CTA is easy to spot and import, and your logo.

Select Share, Download, use the designated size, and use a PNG for the file type.

Results:

The prompt "In 3-dimensional type, have the word ANNOUNCING surrounded by confetti" was entered. Numerous renditions were created, but it took adjusting the words and retrying to finally get something that was close to what was prompted.

The first option for graphics changed the prompt on its own and produced "a cupcake in a pastel color scheme." The next try produced a "metallic colors holographic background." The third try was more photographic.

Finally, a fairly close image was produced when the prompt was shortened to ANNOUNCING surrounded by confetti.

You may have to try different terms to get what you want.

IMAGES 5-8

Canva image options from the above prompts.

USING **FIGMA**

Create files from scratch, import designs from Sketch, or start from templates.

Files are great for collaboration, while your drafts are more personal. If you share them, they're view-only.

To create a BlueSky post using Figma, follow these steps:

First, set up your canvas by opening Figma and starting a new design file. Set the canvas size to 1080x1080 pixels for a square format. To create a post from a template, you need to join a community and then choose a template. Duplicate it and input it into your account to edit.

Next, design your post. Add text using Figma's text tools and customize the font style, size, and color. Insert images by dragging them from your computer into Figma. Use shapes, lines, and other elements for visual accents, arranging text and images aesthetically within the square format.

To fill an existing layer with an image, select the layer and open the Actions menu. Choose "Make an image," enter a prompt, and click "Make it" or press Return.

Then, export your design. Choose PNG or JPEG as the export format and click "Export" to save the image on your computer.

Finally, upload your design to BlueSky. Open the BlueSky app and start a new post, attach the exported image from your device, and add any necessary text or details in the app.

Keep some additional tips in mind: consider BlueSky's character limit when designing text, develop a consistent color palette and design style, and explore Figma community templates for social media posts.

USING **COPILOT**

Creating a social media post using Creator is a fairly easy process. First, sign up for an account on the Creator platform or log in if you already have one.

Select the type of social media post you want to create, such as an image, video, or text post. Input the topic and title of your post, and choose the format you prefer, like image, slides, or video.

Use the AI tool to generate the content for your post, and then edit the design, content, image, video, or audio as needed. Apply your branding elements, such as colors, fonts, backgrounds, and icons, and use features like hierarchy, alignment, and spacing to make the text and graphics clear and readable.

Before posting, preview your design to ensure everything looks perfect and make any necessary adjustments. Finally, share the post directly to your social media account or download it if you have a paid plan. You can ask Copilot for a more detailed design or have it if you have any questions.

USING **GEMINI**

First, create at least three images.

To use Gemini for image creation, enter a prompt that accurately describes the desired image, then click "Create" to receive suggested images. Select an image to insert. To enhance the quality of your images, include details about the subject, setting, and background. Avoid figurative language and provide more comprehensive details in your prompt.

There are some limitations to Gemini image generation. You must agree to Google's Terms of Service, including the Prohibited Use Policy. Do not infringe on others' copyright or privacy rights. Users under 18 are not eligible to use Gemini for generating images. To generate images featuring people, an upgrade to Gemini Advanced is required.

Once you are satisfied with your images, proceed with the actual post design. Open your preferred Google Workspace application (such as Docs) and access the "Help me Write" feature or navigate directly to the Gemini web interface.

When crafting your prompt, clearly specify the subject of your post (e.g., product launch, event announcement, company update), identify your target audience, indicate the desired tone (e.g., informative, humorous, promotional), and mention the platform (Instagram, Twitter, LinkedIn) since different platforms have varying character limits and posting styles.

For example, you might say, "Compose a Facebook post promoting our new summer collection of sunglasses, targeting young adults, with a fun and energetic tone."

After entering your prompt, Gemini will produce a draft social media post with relevant text and potential hashtags. Thoroughly review the generated text, making necessary adjustments to ensure it aligns with your brand voice, messaging, and platform guidelines.

Disclaimer

When using generative AI tools for creating images and designs, the results are generally available for commercial purposes. According to the US Copyright Office (see below), copyright ownership cannot be claimed for any of the images. AI-generated images may infringe on third-party intellectual property rights. Please review the "Generative AI Terms of Use" for any AI tools you utilize.

The US Copyright Office has confirmed that AI-generated material and suggestions are not protected by copyright. In its report, *Copyright and Artificial Intelligence, Part 2: Copyrightability*, the office concluded that "Copyright protects the original expression in a work created by a human author, even if the work also includes AI-generated material." Conversely, copyright does not apply to AI-generated content that includes some human content. The report clarified that from a graphic design standpoint, artificial intelligence is copyrightable if it is used as a tool to style or produce effects in human-generated work. For definitive guidance on your design, consult a copyright attorney. The report is available at: copyright.gov/ai/Copyright-and-Artificial-Intelligence-Part-2-Copyrightability-Report.pdf

1 | (2024, December 10). *Facebook advertising and marketing - statistics & facts*. Statista Research Department. https://www.statista.com/topics/1559/facebook-marketing/#topicOverview

The fundamentals of marketing design

6

Learning Objectives.

The learner will be in a position to simulate what makes viewers look at marketing. They will be prepared to communicate the message. The user will be competent to apply the art of typography.

IMAGE 6-1

Craiyon provides many options on an image of a letter but does not do headlines and multiple letters.

AI Practicum | Craiyon prompt: Script letter in a 3D font that swirls and has filigree in color.

What makes viewers look at marketing

Think about it for a minute —surely you would love people to see your post that need you right now. How often are they going to go searching social media for your company's solution if they need it right away? They are going to call somebody they know for a referral; they will reach out and ask somebody that has used an industry similar to yours, or they will do the easiest and fastest solution — search on the internet. Rarely will they leisurely scroll through posts to find a solution.

For the most part, potential clients are looking at posts for entertainment, updates on people, and information that applies to them. The last thing they want to think about is your company.

However, they may remember your post, and then they will take a few minutes to search for your company post. This is the number one reason for keeping your posts to a certain template-like look—easy to recall, and when they see the new posts, they mentally know it is about your company.

Keep the message easy to remember with simple verbiage and your logo large, and have something that grabs their attention so that they can look at that image and they think of your company. Sure, you would like to have your phone number and website and all that other information but keep it minimal.

Now comes the difficult part. How are you going to create something that is eye-catching, memorable, or creates an action? That's what this book is about. You're going to learn some of the simple basics that graphic designers should know, but not all do. Let's at least get you going in the right direction. Don't expect every post to be a home run. There are too many out there, too many going through it. Try different styles and see what kind of reactions you get. Thumbs-up impressions and comments are all important stats that, if you can track them, give you a direction for your audience.

People look at posts because something in them attracts them. Make sure your marketing does get their attention.

Individuals like something for nothing, so if you can have a save now or buy one, get one free. Giveaways are nice, as well as limited time offers. But it has to be something they're going to want to get. They may not need it in the spring, but that is when you advertise it. In a hot August, the HVAC company will be busy, so there is no reason to advertise offers unless your team does not have any work.

IMAGE 6-2

AI Practicum | Craiyon prompt: Number 5 bursting and colorful.

The image attracts

Bringing focus to the image has two meanings. One explanation is that the image being used in the post is the point of interest for the viewer. The second focus is more subtle. The company brand needs to be the focus of the design, but that does not mean it has to be huge—just legible.

Graphic designers use images either to explain the design or as an eye-catching element. Light, medium, and dark tones will make up the image's values.

Typically, the pictures are classified as either illustrative or photographic. The first choice made when using artificial intelligence to create a picture is whether it is an illustration or a photograph. Photographs are images produced by a camera, but photoreal illustrations are works of art that mimic photographs.

The visual method is used to add depth to an illustration. In an effort to give an item dimension, directional light and a shadow are used. The opposite method is used when an item or subject's articulated shape is a solid or a boundary-delineating texture without a light source.

Cropping is the process of trimming an image's edges to make it fit a specific space or to create an eye-catching visual. For emphasis, you can crop images, drawings, typography, paintings, sketches, and forms. Cropping the artwork can significantly increase its appeal. In visual communications, the designer wants the observer to pause and consider the composition.

Practice and attempting to view the complete image for the "first time" are necessary for this skill. The viewer's attention will be captured right away if the boring sections of an image are creatively removed. Remind yourself that to the viewer, an image is a story. As a marketing designer, you should remember the image also has a single message to emphasize. Options for focusing on the image are to make it have more impact or be more pleasing. Try to create an emotional response by making the image more personal.

The company brand is made up of specific fonts, colors, and an attitude.

To help the viewer remember marketing, stay with the brand style.

IMAGE 6-3

Type has texture

AI Practicum | Pixlr prompt: Filling a page with the words 'no space available.'

The narrative begins

The primary idea behind studying visual design is to center one's attention on the design's purpose. Visual storytelling is the process of conveying information about a service, event, or product through design. The six W's—Who, What, Why, When, Where, and How—are the fundamental issues that every tale must address.

The first consideration for any creative working on a project is always the intended audience. The objective is to captivate and inform the audience using all the graphic designer's resources. It would appear that the graphic designer either forgot or never set out to achieve the intended result in many of today's digital solutions.

Start the creative thinking process by creating a list of the product's or service's positives. Develop your method for analyzing and separating data through observing and identifying various qualities that might have otherwise been overlooked.

By analyzing the attributes of an object, person, place, character, topic or theme, product, or service, one can identify characteristics that may inspire ideas. If you can brainstorm with a group, the results tend to be more out of your comfort level. Stand, sit, walk, move around, and play a game while focusing with others on the creative problem. There are no bad ideas, and someone needs to write all of the ideas down. While they say there are no BAD ideas during this phase, ridiculous ones will deter the process and even cause angst. Try not to censor your ideas. Go ahead and spit out the first ideas that come to mind. Don't solve the complete problem with the ideas — you are just looking for a starting point. Use words first and then images, since images are real and can box in the free flow of ideas.

IMAGE 6-4

Type has texture.

AI Practicum | Fotor prompt: in Pin-Up style, create a headline in circus 3D type with many colors that says, "Welcome to the big top."

Utilize reverse thinking and define how the company solves a customer's problems. Then they show how the previous solutions caused problems or failed. Make sure you explore how solutions can cause your target market to be dissatisfied or frustrated with a service or product.

For instance, for books on artificial intelligence such as this one, publishers have designed covers showing robots. Good or bad idea? Well, if buyers are concerned about losing their jobs to robots, why would they purchase the book?

A compelling social media post narrative should be pertinent to your audience, engaging, and have a clear purpose. A flyer should offer something your target market is interested in buying or using.

A case for type

Marketing designers utilize the term "uppercase" to indicate capital letters and "lowercase" to represent non-capital letters. The cases used to store movable items inspired these terms. When composing a page, the pressman used two compartments to store type. In order to extract letters from the drawer and use them on the press's surface, the printer positioned the cases in a cabinet in front of the press. Before inking, they pulled the letters and placed them in their correct reverse order on the galley. The capital letters were stored in the top drawer since they were used less frequently, resulting in a lighter box. The pressmen used the capitals for brief lines of text, such as headlines. The cabinet was exceedingly heavy due to the quantity of moveable items in the bottom drawer. Therefore, we designate 'lowercase' for non-capital letters and 'uppercase' for capital ones.

Designers must capture the attention of the potential reader in order to entice them to read the content. Utilize a font size for the headline that is the largest or most prominent typeface on the page. Some typefaces are more legible as they are intentionally meant to direct the reader's focus towards the information, rather than being distracting or perceived as overly challenging or time-consuming to read. The fonts that capture a reader's attention are the ones used for headlines and subheadings.

Observe the typeface used this page. The typeface was selected to be easily readable for viewers accustomed to reading long passages. When children are taught to read, they are primarily introduced to lowercase letters with only a few capital letters.

IMAGE 6-5

Examples of Serif fonts. Which letters were created by typesetting and which letter was AI-generated?

AI Practicum | Express prompts: Capital Q and painted with watercolors; small lowercase non-capital letter p carved; Capitol S serif font with 3D and filigree. One font is called Baskerville.

When selecting a typeface, consider its readability and relevance to the page. If a very distinctive typeface causes the viewer to stop and notice the differences from normal fonts, that distinctive font is most likely to be less readable than other options. The ideal typeface for headlines frequently proves ineffective when used as a 10-point font for body content due to its poor readability. To differentiate between a headline font and a body copy font, the designer can simply read it aloud at both a small and large scale. If the text is challenging to read when displayed at a small size, it is probable that it was specifically designed as a display font. Headline fonts can be all capital letters, while text fonts are more effective when used with a combination of upper- and lower-case letters. As a general guideline, display fonts are typically chosen for headlines and should be set at a size of 14 points or larger. Text fonts are utilized for content and are typically set between 6 and 12 points.

IMAGE 6-6

Examples of Sans Serif fonts. Which letters were typeset and which letters were AI-generated?

AI Practicum | Express prompts: Capital H in a serif font coming out of a tunnel in 3 dimensions; small lowercase non-capital letter r floating in space, neon style with art type. Two fonts are called Acumin Pro.

Sans serif fonts are suitable for headlines, particularly when using condensed or compressed variations. Due to the narrower structure of characters in sans serif fonts, they have the ability to increase the height of headlines and create a noticeable difference from the rest of the material. Sans serif typography is characterized by a simple and angular design, including minimal variation in stroke thickness. Designers set type as capitals sparingly to create emphasis on a headline and subconsciously tell the reader to "LOOK AT THIS!" They also keep the line of type short to ensure easy readability.

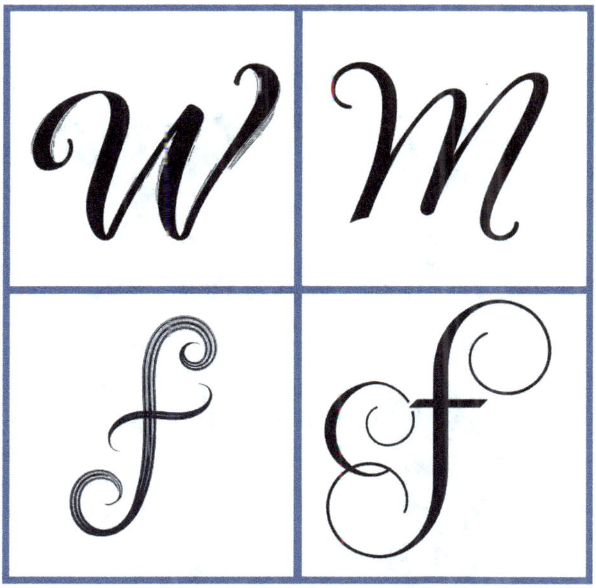

IMAGE 6-7

Examples of Script fonts. Look closely at the typefaces to see which were AI-generated, typeset, and handwritten.

AI Practicum | Express prompts: small lowercase non-capital letter f written with blue-black ink; script w that is written with ink. One font is called Gwendolyn.

Given the ease of designing type on a computer, many creatives tend to overlook the fact that type can also be an image. Before the invention of letters, images served as the primary medium for communication and conveying messages. Illustrators create types based on images. Effective designers are the ones who do not limit themselves to what the computer can type.

When you get to Chapter 14, you will learn how to download free-use fonts, so you do not need to use only the ones that come with a program such as Word or CorelDRAW. You might use AI generators to create images and for the email or printed marketing, type the message yourself if you have a design program.

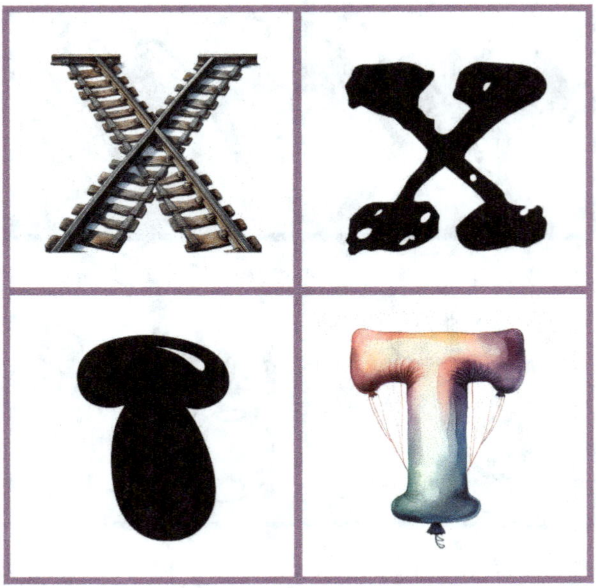

IMAGE 6-8

Examples of Decorative fonts. Deciding the AI and the typeset versions might be more difficult. As a hint one font is called Blow Up, and another font is known as 2010 Pipo Pro.

AI Practicum | Express prompts: small lowercase non-capital letter x made out of tracks; letter T that looks like a balloon.

The art of typography

Use type to create eye-catching images. Many designers draw out a headline, scan the idea, clean it up with artificial intelligence generative software, and drop that image in as the headline. They understand the structure and uniformity required to make this approach viable.

Marketing designers should select appropriate font categories based on readers' perceptions of font styles. A clean sans serif font may appear more modern, inventive, or futuristic to viewers than other font classifications. Serif fonts may be perceived as antiquated, although they are ideal for designs requiring elegance or a traditional aesthetic. Designs that are personal to elegant fall under the script font category, while decorative fonts are considered inventive and attention-grabbing.

In the beginning there was serif

Serif fonts have been used since the printing press was invented around the mid-1400s using moveable type. They emulated the handwriting of that time. The old-style serif has been around for centuries and is still a good choice for text or content.

In a serif typeface family, there will be 'roman' type, which is where the letters are vertical, and 'italic,' which is where the letters slant and have severe thick and thin strokes to stand out and be emphasized. Serif italics are completely redesigned type structures that are almost like another font but based on angles.

The popular Modern Serif has very thin serifs but is not suitable for small sizes. The slab serif is very blocky, which is great for headlines but not easily readable at a small body copy size.

Sans serif typefaces are considered modern

Fonts that do not have serifs are known as sans serif. These faces do not have italics. Instead, these typefaces are slanted so that the type is leaning with basically the same structure. They may have an italic, but it is not a true italic. Since sans serif started being used in the late 1800s, it has been the most popular typeface style since people feel it is more innovative and modern.

Script typefaces are forms of cursive

Fonts that appear handwritten or resemble calligraphy are known as script. This category ranges from delicate type for announcements to rough medieval-style type such as Blackletter, which was used as newspaper banner logos. Now you will see this style used for heavy metal bands.

Decorative typefaces are eye-catching.

The last category, Decorative, is a catch-all for any font style that does not fit into the other 3 categories. Their approaches are distinct and rarely used for body content since decorative typefaces are usually not readable at a small size. Marketers need to remember these are display fonts that function as headlines and starting points for promotional logos. This style can appear sci-fi, historical, techno, grungy, or cartoony. Many have structures that are almost abstract or are rigidly geometric.

The phases of AI marketing design

7

Learning Objectives

The reader will know how to determine the steps to follow for every campaign. They can employ the value of research in their projects and will be capable of breaking down a marketing budget.

IMAGE 7-1

AI Practicum | The same prompt was used for three AI generative image tools: 3 concrete steps leading to the clouds from a down-below forced perspective. 7-1A used Microsoft Creator, 7-1B used Adobe Firefly, and 7-1C used Canva.

Three steps of preparation in every campaign

It seems obvious, but every step of a marketing campaign from creation is important. Here are the basic parts of every successful plan:

Step 1 is updating the company website.

IMAGE 7-2

Sometimes the loading icon is referred to by website developers as the circle of death since web surfers tend to select the back button when they see a website loading with a spinning icon.

Content: So many business owners want to stuff a website with everything that might possibly sell their company's product or service. No one wants to search through a website that is overwhelmingly filled with content. On an average website, visitors will scroll down to see about 50-70% of the page. When a website has too much and makes it work, it causes a viewer to hit the back button and bounce to another option. Search engine robots who index the pages are the exception, but even they do not view a website in its entirety all at once. Searchers are looking for specific answers, and these points need to be obvious and quick reads.

Selling Points: The website should sell why that company is different than the competition and will solve or answer the potential customers concerns. Let them call and have a few questions to ask—that is the salesperson's dream. Remember, over 43% of the viewers for your website are looking at it on a mobile device and will not scroll more than three times.

Speed: This is possibly the main cause of losing visitors. There has been a lot of research into site abandonment, with about 53% of visitors to mobile sites leaving when it takes longer than three seconds to load and 40% on a desktop site.

Understand the importance of the company website. Make sure it is fine-tuned and ready for visitors before your campaign is fully operational.

IMAGE 7-3

AI Practicum | Craiyon prompt: Create an image of a customer magnet. The options were mostly flat art, and your free download was low resolution, suitable for internet use, not print. However, there is a subscription version for higher-quality image downloads.

Step 2 is updating the Google Business Profile.

Customer Magnet: The box on the right side when someone searches your company needs to be up to date. The GBP used to be called Google My Business many years ago, and as a modern marketer, you need to use the correct term. Watch your own reaction when a so-called expert uses the old term and then follows it up with how you need blogs. You know they are not up to date on Google SGE.

Reviews: You need to make sure all the great reviews, especially four- and five-star comments, have a reply. Repeat the name of your company, use the reviewer's name, and thank them and name the service they are referencing. Do not copy-paste generic replies. Potential customers read these and subconsciously rate your company.

Posts: The GBP should be on your list to update news, etc. It is a great area to publicize offers or events.

Step 3 is setting up the social media.

Many business owners rely on posting to social media as their marketing. Considering how many posts and the time they are present; this is not the strongest area of a campaign. It is vital, though, to keep the company account accurate and post on it regularly with interesting information or updates. You need to have a five-subject carousel of posts. See NEETS in Chapter 6.

Your to-do list is extremely long, and you have very little time or budget – where do you turn?

There are six platform posts, three article publishing websites, and a three-touch print campaign with printing, gathering addresses, targeting the creative elements of a design, and placing the posts.

The content and images must not infringe on copyrights held by other sources. The easiest option is to create your own images and write your own content. As the originator, you can make sure the content and images work together and focus on your target market. However, sometimes you should use it to save you time and speed up the process. Copy-paste the AI-generated content into a writing assistant and use the rephrase or rewrite tool. Then run a check for plagiarism.

Make sure that none of the images you use violate copyright regulations. You will need to locate high-quality stock photos if you do not have your own images. Additionally, you must determine which available tools can improve the way you appear on social media.

You also need to make sure that the sizes of your images on social media are appropriate. First presentations must maintain a professional appearance. While producing visual content for social media, social media marketers must get a lot of things right. Creating the correct size is really important for a number of reasons:

- Pixelation causes the viewer to assume the image quality equals the quality of the presentation.
- Stretched or compressed images also reflects on your message—amateur or professional product.
- Each social media platform's feed will be optimized for your images. This can help increase engagement.
- It allows the viewer to see the entire image. Incorrect sizing could cut off some of your brand's messaging.

Successful marketing starts with research

Market research measures the effectiveness of marketing campaigns, helping businesses make data-driven decisions about resource allocation and strategy adjustments. It helps them understand their target market, identify consumer needs and preferences, and make informed choices.

The data from this research can be used for product development, pricing, distribution, and promotional strategies. It reveals demographics and psychographics of potential customers, enabling effective targeting and tailored marketing strategies. Research identifies new market opportunities, emerging trends, changes in consumer behavior, and shifts in the competitive landscape.

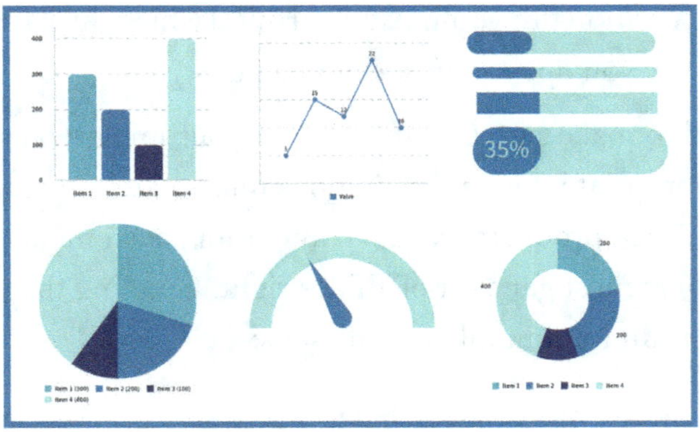

IMAGE 7-4

AI Practicum | Adobe Express has a Charts and Grids option to create research results with bar charts, line charts, pie charts, progress bars, progress donuts, and gauges.

Understanding market trends and consumer behaviors from research allows businesses to develop strategies and innovative products that meet unmet needs. It also helps differentiate from competitors and reduce risks by providing data-driven insights, preventing costly mistakes.

Improving marketing effectiveness is a key goal. By understanding customer needs, businesses can enhance products and services, leading to higher satisfaction and loyalty. Effective marketing campaigns resonate with target audiences, avoiding wasted resources.

Pricing strategies are developed based on customer willingness to pay and competitor pricing. Marketing research ensures informed business decisions, reducing risks.

Small businesses can use affordable methods like surveys, focus groups, competitor analysis, social media engagement, and interviews to gather valuable information. Tracking website traffic and user behavior provides insights into customer interests.

Combining these methods helps small businesses make informed decisions and improve marketing strategies. Once research results are compiled, create a campaign using keywords, phrases, images, and AI options to best fit the target market.

Small business research tools

Small businesses can conduct marketing research using various methods that are both affordable and effective. These tools offer a variety of features to suit different needs, ranging from simple surveys to more complex data collection and analysis. Utilizing existing data from industry reports, market studies, and government publications can save time and provide valuable information about market trends and demographics.

Surveys and questionnaires are cost-effective ways to gather information from your target audience. Organizing small groups to discuss products or services, or utilizing social media posts to engage with customers, can provide valuable insights into consumer preferences and opinions.

Studying competitors to understand their strengths and weaknesses can help identify opportunities and threats in the market. Gathering feedback from social platforms and engaging with the audience can also assist in monitoring trends and consumer sentiment.

Artificial intelligence can be helpful but always check the findings for accuracy. Since ChatGPT, Creator, and Gemini pull their findings from the internet, they can give you a general basis of results, but it can be slanted based upon the sources.

One of the best but most time-consuming research methods is conducting one-on-one interviews with potential customers. While this data can be collected via phone, face-to-face interactions in informal settings can yield more in-depth, honest, and detailed feedback, helping to better understand customer needs and preferences.

Upon tabulating research results, the process of creating a campaign begins. Generate a list of keywords and phrases that resonate with the research findings. Subsequently, compile images and explore AI options with prompts. Apply content to the images and evaluate which approach aligns best with the target market. Once a campaign is live, tracking website traffic and user behavior can provide insights into customer interests and interactions with the website.

Experienced marketers recognize the importance of comprehensive research. By combining these methods, small businesses can gather extensive data to make informed decisions and improve marketing strategies.

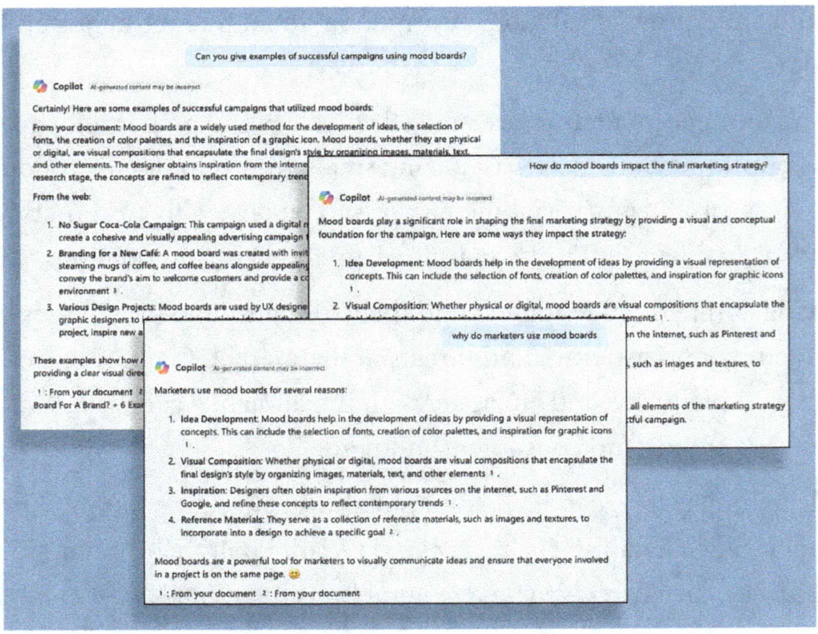

IMAGE 7-5

AI Practicum | In a Microsoft Word document using Copilot, prompted: Why do marketers use mood boards? How do mood boards impact the final marketing strategy? Can you give examples of successful campaigns using mood boards?

The role of mood boards in marketing design

Marketers use mood boards in marketing research to visualize and communicate brand identity, target audience preferences, and the overall aesthetic direction for campaigns, products, or services, facilitating better understanding and alignment among stakeholders.

Many creatives are visually oriented, and building a mood board translates abstract concepts like brand personality and values into a tangible visual representation, making it easier to communicate the brand's identity.

By collecting images, colors, fonts, patterns, textures, and styles that resonate with the target audience and represent the brand's personality, mood boards help marketers gain insights into their preferences and desired aesthetic. Mood boards serve as a visual language, allowing marketers to communicate their ideas and vision more effectively with clients, designers, and other team members.

Creatives are always looking for inspiration and new ideas on how to approach product marketers. Mood boards can spark creativity and generate new ideas for marketing campaigns, product designs, or visual communication strategies.

Mood boards should not be limited to images. They can have very short three- to five-word phrases, past color palettes, and the brand's past campaigns. As the board is built, the marketer should refer to the consumer responses.

Types of mood boards in marketing research.

Mood boards are a widely used method for the development of ideas, the selection of fonts, the creation of color palettes, and the inspiration of a graphic icon. Mood boards, whether they are physical or digital, are visual compositions that encapsulate the final design's style by organizing images, materials, text, and other elements. At the research stage, the concepts are refined to reflect contemporary trends. There are numerous types of mood boards based on the subject or goal.

Campaign Mood Board: The visual direction of a marketing campaign, ensuring consistency and effectiveness.

Target Audience Mood Board: Understands the visual preferences, lifestyles, and interests of the target audience.

Brand Identity Mood Board: Defines and visualizes a brand's core values, style, and target audience.

Competitive Analysis Mood Board: Analyzes the visual style and messaging of competitors, identifying opportunities for differentiation.

If you use Copilot to generate content, one intersecting inclusion is where Copilot found the information it used to write the content. In the example Image 7-4, note the websites the Copilot information used. It is one of the few AI-generative content tools that cites its sources.

11 Inspiring Mood Board Examples: Step-by-Step Guide—Maze

What is a Mood Board For A Brand? + 6 Examples—Dream Farm Agency

IMAGE 7-6

AI Practicum | DeepAI image generator with the prompt: Show a hundred-dollar bill being stretched across and around a computer.

Setting up a budget

Here is an overview of creating a marketing budget.

Initially, define the marketing objectives and anticipated outcomes. Following this, it is essential to conduct thorough research on the target audience to comprehend their needs and preferred communication channels. Next, audit your existing marketing efforts to identify what's working and what isn't, and estimate costs for each potential marketing tactic across various channels like social media, email, content marketing, and paid advertising. Estimate the costs for each potential marketing strategy across various channels such as social media, email, content marketing, and paid advertising. Finally, allocate the budget based on expected return on investment (ROI) and continuously monitor performance to make adjustments as necessary. Finally, allocate your budget based on expected ROI and regularly monitor performance to adjust as needed.

Here is a breakdown of establishing a budget.

Developing the expenses associated with a marketing campaign sounds simple, but the failure is in the details. Guessing is different than estimating. One is based on experience, and one is based on wishful thinking.

1. Set clear marketing goals such as increasing brand awareness, lead generation, or sales. Remember to apply S.M.A.R.T.

2. Identify who you are trying to reach with your marketing message by understanding their demographics, interests, pain points, and online behavior.

3. Review your research on market trends and competitor marketing. Include your analysis of their strategies, strengths, and weaknesses to identify opportunities.

4. Select the platforms where your target audience spends their time and break down and calculate the cost for each channel.

a. Advertising costs and boosted post fees should be available.

b. For videos and podcasts, you may want to set up a range for production.

c. Graphic design and website development should be figured per project to save you from going over budget.

5. Now comes the difficult part of budgeting. What is the ROI potential that will be generated? Rank the media channels from most expensive to best value. Choose three options with the goal of creating a low-cost, medium-cost, and expensive approach.

6. Include the highest return on investment potential for each estimate.

7. Present it to the financial approver if at all possible—do not email it.

Marketing design uses both sides of the brain

8

Learning Objectives

In this chapter, the reader will know how to paraphrase memorable marketing concepts. They will competently relate visual theories in marketing design. The learner will be qualified to distinguish how viewers react to colors.

IMAGE 8-1

AI Practicum | Adobe Firefly prompt: bright blue Chevrolet Camaro going fast down the highway with a zoom effect on the image to show speed.

Know the audience before starting

For marketers, social media is another stage for company press releases, product news, and service updates to achieve interaction with existing customers and potential customers. The medium is a strong method to present effective messages. However, marketers need to make sure posts and ads look professional but not generic and that they are placed on the correct platform with the proper message for that target market.

This book will briefly go through graphic art basics such as how to choose a color palette (not by personal likes and dislikes), font choices (not just what is at the top of the list on your computer), and what creates compelling design.

It is common sense that if you are trying to communicate, you need to know who you are speaking to, so you know what terminology to use. For example, if you are designing a flyer handout for a higher education symposium, you will use an academic or formal voice, with two- and three-syllable words and compound sentences. A flyer directed at teenage boys will use a different style of narrative with four or five letter words and short sentences on a subject they are interested in stopping texting to look at.

Company logo design–don't be tempted

A company spends a large amount of the marketing budget money promoting and reinforcing its brand name. Do not try to pinch pennies as a marketer by designing the logo yourself — hire a professional. If you can afford it, have them provide a style guide to go with the logo. They have years of education and experience in logo design. To design it yourself, even with AI, or expect to go to a website and spend $25 and receive a memorable, iconic logo that resonates with your target market is not reasonable. It would be tantamount to a graphic designer without any marketing education and training trying to develop a full-scale successful marketing campaign.

However, if you are creative, you can design a logo for an event, a special promotion, a celebratory post, and trade show graphics. The main reason you may want to try to design promotional logos is if it flops, it will not be around long, and since it did not cost much except your time, you can learn and move on to the next design. If it is well received and memorable, then you are a marketing designer.

This book will explain color and fonts enough that you can develop these kinds of promotional logos. After all, you have the talent—you are just not trained yet.

A guide for creating memorable marketing

The key to memorable marketing is knowing your target, developing a distinctive brand narrative, employing eye-catching imagery, and producing emotionally charged content.

Spend time getting to know your target audience. Determine their wants, needs, and areas of discomfort. Have answers for the issues they encounter. List their demographics, including their time-consuming interests. If they spend their time online, create an email, message, and social media campaign. With this information, you can customize your message in your marketing.

Define the brand.

Construct a message with meaning and purpose. Determine the USP (unique selling proposition) of your brand and the reasons why consumers should pick you over your rivals. Create a distinctive voice for your brand that can be authoritative, serious, or playful. Think about the subtle way the tone will evoke an emotional reaction in your audience. Ensure a consistent visual identity on all platforms. Choose a recognizable and eye-catching logo, color scheme, and typeface.

Focus on the narrative that has a complementary image.

People relate to stories, so use them to spread the word about your brand while maintaining visually appealing content that is pertinent to your brand. Your content can be more engaging if it contains high-quality photos and videos. Provide your audience with something they can learn from or use. Make sure your content is easy to share and digest.

Use a variety of formats, such as blog posts, videos, infographics, and social media updates. Engage with your audience through effective communication techniques. People are more likely to remember something that makes them laugh, cry, or feel something. People can spot fake or inauthentic marketing efforts a mile away.

Don't be afraid to repeat your message.

Your target market needs to see your brand and message multiple times before they truly remember it. Use a variety of channels to reach your audience. Don't rely on just one or two channels. Track your results and make adjustments as needed, and test ways to improve your marketing efforts.

IMAGE 8-2

AI Practicum | Deep AI prompt: Show 5 people close together in the foreground and in the distance 2 people not near them in a parking lot.

Visual theories in marketing design

Until the early 1900s, psychologists, graphic artists, and marketers believed that the most effective method of conveying a message was to cram as much information as possible onto a page, with the expectation that individuals would read it in its entirety. The theory was founded on structuralism, which claimed that elements carried no value in separation. The individual aesthetics were not perceived by humans; rather, they perceived the overall structured system as a collection of elements in relation to other elements.

IMAGE 8-3

AI Practicum | This example uses the same verbiage as 8-2. Fotor AI Image Generator prompt: Show 5 people close together in the foreground and in the distance 2 people not near them in a parking lot

A group of psychologists proposed that individuals perceive the individual components of a layout that collectively form complete patterns. They conducted experiments to test this hypothesis in the domains of perception, learning, and comprehension. The Gestalt Principles, which are the results, serve as the foundation for effective visual design communication. The three principles to focus on are figure-ground, proximity, and similarity.

"Proximity" is the term used to describe the principles that govern how individuals see visual items in relation to the arrangement of those objects. There is a tendency for individuals to interpret objects that are in close proximity to one another as belonging to a shared group. The spatial proximity or nearness of things can affect how we organize visual information into coherent patterns or groups.

IMAGE 8-4

AI Practicum | This example uses the same verbiage as 8-3. Dalle-E prompt: Show 5 people close together in the foreground and in the distance 2 people not near them in a parking lot

As you try different AI tools to generate an image to illustrate the point, you will see which ones seem to understand the prompt more than the others. Take notes so you will know which ones to use for a certain look or output. You will discover some are better at certain types of solutions, but all seem to have strong points.

There is a concept called the "similarity principle" that states that when two or more things are similar to one another, viewers may perceive them as a group or arrangement. Individual components can achieve a coherent visual representation. Several items may share similarities in their shape, color, size, texture, or value. These similarities can also take on different forms. It is logically possible to establish unity when the various components share a greater degree of similarity with one another. Marketing designers have the ability to utilize the idea of similarity in order to draw attention to something that is distinct inside a layout.

IMAGE 8-5

AI Practicum | This example uses the same verbiage as 8-4. Dalle-E prompt: Show 5 people close together in the foreground and in the distance 2 people not near them in a parking lot

The human eye is able to differentiate between various objects based on their background, the region that surrounds them, their form, their silhouette, or their dimensions. Figure Ground operates on the basis of this principle. Maintaining the appropriate equilibrium between the subject in the foreground and the backdrop not only attracts attention but also generates a layout that is visually appealing by playing with contrast. Through the use of overlapping items, forms, or type, a layout can give the impression of providing more space. Long objects or features closer to the observer can appear larger and give the scene depth by dramatically shrinking them. To give a layout depth, place larger pieces in front of background elements. The saturation of color and value creates a sense of spaciousness. When we look further into the distance at mountains, the value and intensity of color get progressively less intense.

IMAGE 8-6

AI Practicum | This example uses the same verbiage as 8-5. Microsoft Creator prompt: Show 5 people close together in the foreground and in the distance 2 people not near them in a parking lot

Coloring time is the fun time

As a kindergartner, coloring time was a fun time. It should be even more fun for the marketer since no one will complain if they do not follow the rules. One way to build a color palette is to sample the image with an eyedropper tool. This type of palette builds a harmonious color relationship with the image. Colors for highlights stand out and are used sparingly to grab the viewer's attention.

Color should be visually appealing and significantly influence potential customers. Emotional responses may be induced by the values and combinations of tints. The marketing artist wants the target market to feel a connection with the color and not think of the hue as a mix of pigments. The colors established by the branding of the company will create a recognizable identity, which makes it easy for the designer to choose colors.

The amount of research on book colors is astounding. For instance, Printivity Insights has current trends of bestselling book cover colors: Mystery uses black and gray; Romance soft colors such as pink, red, purple, and white; Fantasy is predominately purple, blue, green, silver, and gold; Sci-fi covers are black, gray, red, green, and purple; Horror, unsurprisingly, is red and black; Nonfiction can be blue, red, yellow, black, and white.[1]

Studies have shown the power of color. For instance, in University of Loyola, Maryland research, color was found to increase brand recognition up to 80%. In a comparison of black and white advertisements with the same ads in color, discovered that color designs were read up to 42% more.[2]

On the color wheel, colors opposite each other, such as blue and orange and violet and yellow complement each other. Complementary colors work with any colors opposite on the color wheel, so red orange is opposite blue green. These tend to intensify each other visually.

By choosing colors that work well together, your design will be more cohesive. They provide the most contrast. Use one as the main color and one as the accent.

By varying the colors so that red is a little more on the violet side of the color wheel and adding black or white, you can get a dynamic color wheel. Increasing saturation will make a color brighter and the combination can be energetic.

Value is the range of darkness or lightness of a color. When mixing pigments, to change the value of a color you can add black to make it darker, and white to make it lighter. A darker color is known as a shade and a lighter color is referred to as a tint.

Warm colors such as reds, oranges, and yellows are associated with fire and sunlight and are considered warm hues. Cool colors such as violets, blues and greens are associated with ice, water, and crisp salads. These hues are referred to as cool colors. To achieve contrast with color, the designer can place shades and tints together. Another option is to adjust the saturation and place bright and dull intensity hues together. An easy contrast is using complementary warm and cool colors. Using a large or dominating area of a cool color positioned with small highlights or warm colors creates a pleasing contrast to viewers. The proportion is not always easy to find.

IMAGE 8-7

AI Practicum | NightCafe prompt: rainbow made up of earth tones and pastels.

The color callout in 4-color (CMYK) printing begins with the order in which the press will print the project: Cyan, followed by Magenta, Yellow, and Black, and the percentage of each ink in the color. For instance, a Candy Red would be 10C/100M/90Y/0K. The symbol "K" represents black, while "C" represents cyan. While some professionals contend that the "K" means "key color," the actual definition of the key color refers to the most prominent color used in the design. In order for trim and bleed marks to be visible on each color plate, the lines, as well as registration marks and fold marks, have to be in all four colors at 100%.

When a graphic artist imports their color palette, they will modify the colors to achieve their design objective. InDesign enables the creation of palettes that include earth tones, festive tints, and luxurious colors. An earth-tone color palette is characterized by natural or neutral shades, including brown, green, gray, and red, and is inspired by nature. In addition to their association with specific holidays, festive hues are also indicative of celebrations and gatherings.

The colors are, as a result, intense, vibrant, and forceful. Black with a trace of blue may be a choice, as luxurious colors signify elegance and sophistication. Metallics, such as warm gold, reddish copper, and a cool silver, will elevate whites and purples. Color theory and research form the foundation of the attributes method.

IMAGE 8-8

AI Practicum | This example uses the same verbiage as 8-7. Deep Dream Generator prompt: rainbow made up of earth tones and pastels, Artistic style.

Understanding how we feel about color

Experienced marketers know that just because they like or dislike a color, everyone else does too. It is good to know some basic color theory before establishing a color palette. Marketing designers can create stronger, eye-catching visuals in their layouts with an understanding of how viewers are affected by their past reactions to color and why they make decisions based on color. In UX/UI design, color selection is essential for accessibility, product design, and branding. Color psychology is used in marketing to influence how customers act and view goods.

Cool colors have some blue in them and recede into the background. Warm colors have some yellow or red in them and come toward the viewer. A design will need to use a larger amount of a cool color in the design to have a more dramatic impact than the more dynamic warm colors. Warm colors are usually bright and jump off the page. Therefore, a layout only needs a small number of warm colors to make a dramatic impact.

Red may indicate danger or attraction, while green may indicate safety. These colors elicit automatic reactions. Personal experiences and cultural background have a big impact on how we see and respond to color, which shapes our feelings and tastes. Individual memories and experiences can have a significant impact on our feelings regarding particular colors.

IMAGE 8-9

AI Practicum | This example uses the same verbiage as 8-8. Dall-E prompt: rainbow made up of earth tones and pastels

The colors orange, yellow, and red are frequently linked to energy, excitement, and stimulation. Blue, green, and purple are generally associated with serenity, relaxation, and concentration.

Here is a short guide to color but remember there are exceptions. Think of a bright, electric blue color. It is not a calming, serene hue, but it is considered a cool color—especially if you have it on a supercharged Camaro ZL1.

- Red symbolizes passion, love, fervor, rage, and peril.
- Orange represents happiness, zeal, inventiveness, and coziness.
- Yellow embodies energy, optimism, hope, and happiness.
- Pink is young, feminine, invigorating, and playful.
- Green reflects growth, tranquility, peace, and nature.
- Blue indicates professionalism, trust, loyalty, and melancholy.
- Purple feels serene, cool, and spiritual.

1 | White, J. V. (1997). Color for Impact. Strathmoor Press.

2 | Wiley, N. (2023, March 13). Eye-Catching Book Cover Colors That Sell Best. Printivity Insights. www.printivity.com/insights/2022/12/09/book-cover-colors-that-sell- best

AI for internet marketing solutions

9

Learning Objectives.

The student is going to be in a position to explain advertising requirements for social media. They should be capable of managing a social media post ad campaign. The reader is expected to show how to choose the best social media AI generator.

Starting a social media post ad campaign

It is likely that your company lacks the resources or time to advertise in every potential target market. One feasible approach is to broaden the current consumer base to attract a larger audience. You need a way to include the current followers and use paid advertising.

Social media posts are a method of informing potential consumers about your company and industry information that they may find interesting. Advertising is a powerful tool for promoting your company's brand and encouraging potential consumers to take action.

When designing the ad, think about how you can use a strong image or headline. Stay with your brand colors and make sure the call to action stands out and is easy to access. Remember K.I.S.S. for your title and content. Viewers are not there to read ads but to read posts.

Image carousels, also known as sliders, are elements on web pages that display multiple images or content items in a rotating sequence. A slider shows one slide at a time, while a carousel displays several slides simultaneously.

This chapter does not teach how to set up an advertisement campaign. That process encompasses bidding, identifying your target market, determining the optimal posting times, and deciding on the best placement. Setting up a measurable call to action and defining criteria is not the design's focus. However, marketers are expected to understand how to create such a campaign.

Before you begin, you should determine your target audience and the goal of your campaign. Please ensure that your plan aligns with the appropriate platform for that audience. Write down your ideas for the writing voice you want to use in phrases. Many successful creatives develop a target character that includes some visual descriptions but primarily focuses on the character's identity, hobbies, enjoyment, place of employment, and where they live and eat. This character-building information will help you see them as real people and not just words.

Use a relevant image from your library or stock photos as inspiration for creating attention-grabbing headlines and ad content. Before publishing any sales copy, you should always use a grammar and spelling checker, such as Microsoft Word, or you can use a content generator. Remember to include the company logo, CTA, expiration date, and color scheme of the campaign in the list of requirements for the advertisement.

Marketers overlook YouTube in their campaigns if they are not developing video advertisements to run within the video posts.

Static display ads can seamlessly complement video content or be integrated within in-feed video ads. These ads can feature striking images, compelling text, or a creative blend of both elements. Explore additional advertising options such as bumper, masthead, in-feed, and between-feed placements.

Video advertisements may appear before, during, or after YouTube videos. Aside from the video content, non-video advertisements consist of banner ads and text. However, premium ads are a hybrid of the two, incorporating banner elements and a video.

Considering your target demographic, YouTube display advertisements may be the most effective method to engage with them. If you seek videos but encounter budgetary or scheduling limitations that prevent contracting, AI can generate videos for you—refer to Chapter 13 for further information.

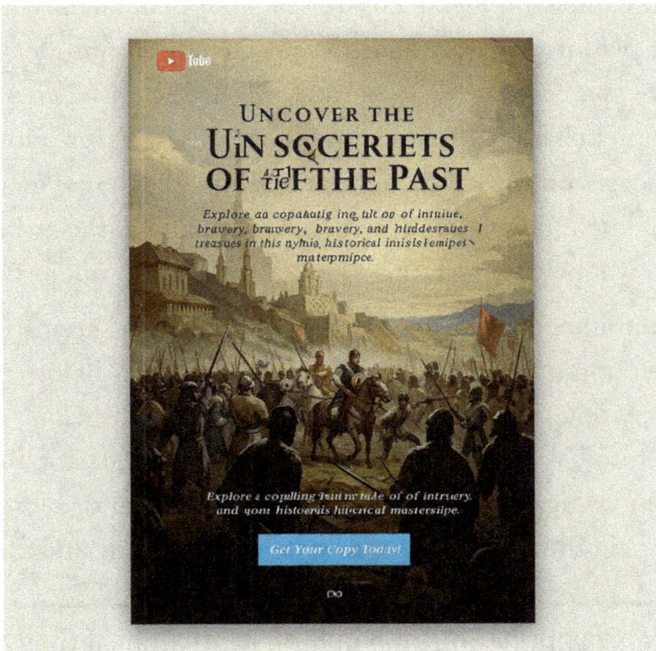

IMAGE 9-1

AI Practicum | Gemini prompt 1: Provided details about the book ad for YouTube.

Google is everywhere but…

Google Gemini was asked, "Can you create a display ad? For YouTube?" The answer was, "Okay, let's craft a compelling YouTube display ad! To help me tailor it perfectly, I need some information from you. Please provide details about…" Gemini asked good questions such as, "What are the key features and benefits?" It also wanted to know details such as "Who is your target audience?" The subject was this book, Marketing Design Using AI. Based on the answers, it developed a scenario listing key features, benefits, target audience, text approaches, and visuals. Gemini recognized the importance of crafting a static image and supplied it with the necessary dimensions. A headline, body text, and a CTA button featuring the caption "Early Bird Discount" were provided. The AI assistant even detailed the process of transforming an image into a video ad.

IMAGE 9-2

AI Practicum | Gemini prompt 2: Can you create the YouTube ad without showing the book cover?

Regrettably, there was no option available to upload an image of the book cover, leading to Gemini creating a new book cover as a replacement. The layout presented in image 9-1 is a book cover rather than an advertisement. The book cover displayed the headline and other elements in small type. An ad should have a large type to capture your interest and a smaller type to sell to you. The ad content should be sales copy and not appear to be a book summary.

At this time, Google Gemini may not be the ideal AI generator for producing visual marketing content. Observe that it is unable to spell 'YouTube' accurately. Research indicates that the top social media ad creators include Adobe Express, Canva, and Figma.

How to choose the best social media AI generator

Previous chapters have discussed the multitude of options for AI generators capable of producing posts. You need an AI tool that focuses on generating images easily and quickly. It should help you create eye-catching content to increase brand visibility. First and foremost, the platform should be easy to use and not too technical.

The AI generator tool of your choice should allow you to easily adjust the narrative tone, style, and content to match your brand identity. It should offer various options for typefaces, color themes, and palettes.

Your posts will require unique images for social media posts. Your printed projects will need high-quality and high-resolution images. The social posts should be correctly sized for your campaign. It should seamlessly adapt your posts for the different platforms where you can easily alter the narrative and voice. It should have intriguing memes and the ability to add hashtags.

Your flyers and direct mail must encompass all necessary elements, and they should allow for the quick upload of your company logo. The solutions should strike a balance, avoiding both a cluttered appearance and an overly sparse look. The text must be easy to read. If the text is too small to read, it might not be a worthwhile investment of your time.

Before you subscribe to one or two, try them out. See how they look when posted. Take the time to evaluate free trials to see which platform best aligns with your goals and workflow.

Canva, Figma, and Express share notable similarities in their approach to responsive design. Adhere to the steps outlined on Express and subsequently implement them across the other platforms. You will notice several differences, as detailed below.

IMAGE 9-3

An Adobe Express template was found after searching for a book ad; the results were a book sale poster. It was sized for Instagram.

Express is available at no cost and offers various resources. Canva necessitates a subscription, which includes a free trial option. Figma offers a desktop version, and its full plan comes with a subscription cost.

Many screens show the view is 100%. When the ad is measured, it usually is not at actual size but closer to 50% larger. Adjust the screen view so you can get an accurate idea of the size of the type. For example, on a high-resolution monitor, the setting is at 33%, while on a no-name brand monitor, it is adjusted to 25%. The duration will appear brief, so make adjustments for the perspective.

We demonstrated ChatGPT 3.5 and its lack of image generation, but ChatGPT 4.0, which is subscription-based, can create strong visuals. It can write content and even recommend a Canva template to use. ChatGPT is good for brainstorming as are Gemini, Claude, and Goblin.

DEMONSTRATION WITH **ADOBE EXPRESS**

If you decide not to create an image with Express but want to upload an image, resize it to the approximate dimensions. A little larger than the actual size is better than smaller, but its size is essential for setting the type.

Select the Instagram Square Post ad from the Express dashboard. Choose the headline and modify it to "Step Into the Future of Social Posts." The left menu provides options for condensing the type and selecting various fonts, along with adjustments for type size.

In the material included in "For marketers and small businesses." To move the type and adjust its angle, if necessary, simply double-click on the moving tool icon. Simply double-click on any items you no longer need and select the trash can option. If you accidentally delete something, you have the option to undo it.

To adjust letter spacing, select the text, navigate to the "Format" panel, and find the "Character Spacing" option to increase or decrease the space between characters. The leading, which refers to the space between lines, can also be adjusted here. Please navigate to the layers and unlock the background. When you double-click on it, you can adjust the darkness in the format menu.

To create a button with a link in the Formatting menu, type "button" and then select one. Enter your type, and then right-click, select the link option, and enter the full URL.

Then download or select the option to post it. You can also resize it if you need it for a print piece.

IMAGE 9-4

Edited Adobe Express template with Express tools to create Instagram ad.

DEMONSTRATION WITH **CANVA**

From the Canva icon dashboard, select social media by scrolling to the right. Select Facebook Post—Landscape, and, similar to Express, find a template and edit the elements to create your ad.

Using the Formatting menu, select text and then add the content that applies. Scroll down on the menu, and you will find interesting options for type styling. When you click on tools, they appear on the left and on the top.

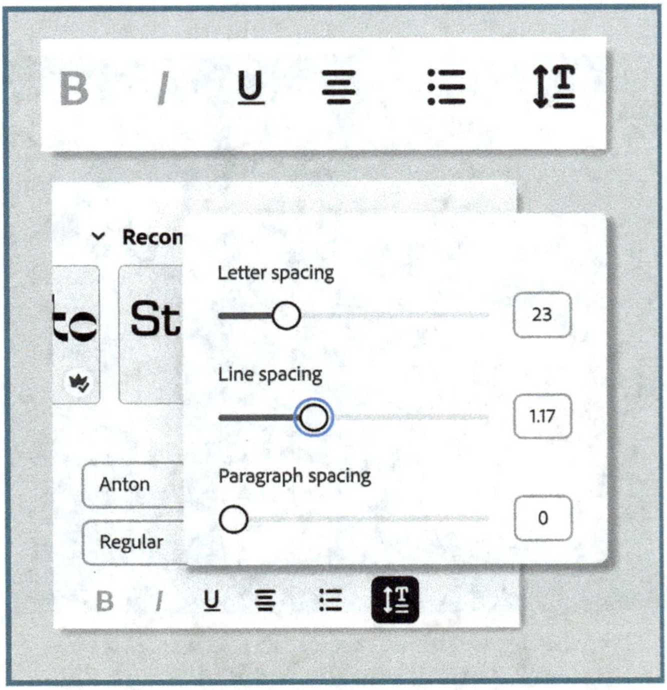

IMAGE 9-5

Logos, color schemes, and images are simple to upload. The tools for text editing are easier to use on Canva than on Express—they are not hidden.

Advertising requirements for social media.

The following list provides an overview of the specifications for some popular social media platforms. This lets you use AI tools to use what you create rather than just going through the motions. Some of these social media platforms allow you to advertise and extend your campaign to your target market. There are too many to put in every medium, and you should check them to make sure they have not changed before you build your ads. See video specs in Chapter 13.

IMAGE 9-6

AI Practicum | Facebook Template example on Canva with prompt: inspector software ad with space for additional content.

Facebook image sizes for ads and carousels:

Image Ads

Size (Width x Height): 1,200 x 628 pixels

Max file size: 30 MB

File type: png, jpg

Carousel Cards

Number: 2 to 10

Size (Width x Height): 1080 x 1080 pixels

Text: 125 characters

LinkedIn image sizes for ads and carousels:

Image Ads

Size (Width x Height): 1,200 x 628 pixels

Max file size: 5 MB

File type: png, jpg

Carousel Cards

Number: 2 to 10

Size (Width x Height): 1080 x 1080 pixels

Title: 255 characters

Description: 255 characters

Pinterest image sizes for ads and carousels:

Size (Width x Height): 1000 x 1000 pixels, 1000 x 1500 pixels.

Max file size: 20 MB on desktop, 32 MB on the app.

File type: png, jpeg, jpg

Carousel Cards

Number: 2 to 5

Size (Width x Height): 1000 x 1500 pixels, 1000 x 1000 pixels

Max file size: 20 MB

Title: 100 characters

Description: 500 characters

Snapchat ad image sizes for ads and carousels:

Static images

Size (Width x Height): 1080 x 1920 pixels.

Max file size: 5 MB for images

File type: png, jpeg, jpg

TikTok image sizes for ads and carousels:

Static images: 2-35 for carousels

Size (Width x Height): 1080 x 1920 pixels.

Max file size: Less than 50 MB

File type: png, jpeg, jpg

Instagram image sizes for ads and carousels:

Static images

Size (Width x Height): 1080 x 1080 pixels.

Max file size: 30 MB for images

File type: png, jpeg, jpg

Carousel Cards

Number: 2 to 10

Size (Width x Height): 1080 x 1080 pixels

YouTube image sizes for ads and carousels:

Image Ads

Size (Width x Height): 300x60, 300x250, 336x280

Max file size: 150 MB

File type: png, jpg

Carousel Cards

Number: 2 to 10

Size (Width x Height): 1080x1080, Landscape 1920x1080, Portrait 1080x1920.

Max file size: 1256MB

File type: mpeg-2, mpeg-4

Headline: 32 characters

Text: 18 characters plus CTA

Static ads that appear during the video are known as In-Feed Ads. They must include an image thumbnail, a headline, and up to two lines of text. Ads that are between video feeds are referred to as Feed Short Ads.

AI for simple print marketing promotions

10

Learning Objectives

By the end of this chapter, the student will be prepared to apply the parts of a design, and they will understand layout guidelines. The user will be in a position to set sales content limits.

IMAGE 10-1

AI Practicum | DeepAI prompt: image of a used vacuum salesman trying to get in the front door. Note the elements around the man are clear and have dimension. The man is in soft focus, which was DeepAI decision.

Do not sell something to be more than it is

Numerous Realtors have acquired the ability to utilize Photoshop and will capture photographs of houses, subsequently adjusting the saturation and luminosity to generate unrealistic images. They induce a luminosity in the green vegetation and an iridescent blue hue in the sky. The potential buyer is eager to view the property, but they are unaware of the reason for their attraction.

They are disappointed upon viewing the property, as it has subconsciously lost its appeal. It does not match the picture in their mind. The actual house is considerably more subdued.

Consequently, the buyer will be dissatisfied before they view the inside of the property. It is important to avoid selling an item for something it is not. Some Realtors contend that they just want to get the buyer to a property, and from that point on, they can sell it.

However, the Realtor® is confronted with an insurmountable battle if the marketing sets unrealistic expectations, and the property lacks curb appeal. This method is applicable to the majority of industries and services that employ marketing.

Sell your company brand for those that will need your company in the future–not for those that need you now.

Another example is savings offers. For example, a dentist opened up recently in the area and sent out postcards to local residents with an EEDM® (C1) with a grand opening special offer. In an attempt to bring in new clients, the first teeth cleaning with an exam and x-rays was for the low price of $79. That was a huge savings since the regular price was $373 with the offer expiring in 30 days.

The goal was to create an offer that potential patients would jump at even though they would have to switch from their existing dentist and face potential pain with a new hygienist.

Problem #1: The call to action focused on the cost of $79, which would be a huge savings. A Google AI generative search resulted in the average costs in the area for adult teeth cleaning with an exam and x-rays being $183. But what about the next time—$373 was more than the going rate in the area. The first visit is a deal, but after that it gets pretty costly.

Problem #2: No real deadline — no real reason to decide quickly. In an attempt to save money and not have to print more postcards, the marketer tried to create a sense of urgency with an expiration but without an actual date. It was meaningless.

Parts of design

It is essential for a marketing designer to have a fundamental understanding of the principles of visual design. The following list includes methods used in compositions to engage the viewer. These methods illustrate elements that are not only visually appealing but also effectively convey ideas.

IMAGE 10-2

AI Practicum | NightCafe prompt: closeup of a grey cat's yellow eyes looking at blue ball of yarn in a dark spooky kitchen.

Contrast

This technique is the most effective method for engaging an audience. Designers employ contrast to distinguish between elements. By employing color, size, texture, and shape, they can establish a complementary layout that prevents the reader from proceeding to the subsequent marketing message. For instance, the text is more prominently displayed when the headline is bold and the background is muted, which draws the viewer's attention to the critical information.

Emphasis

By creating a layout with a certain element that is the most prominent, it creates focal points that immediately capture attention. Designers achieve emphasis by adjusting scale, color, or positioning so that the main element dominates without overwhelming the rest of the layout. Such an approach helps communicate the hierarchy of information clearly.

Movement

Closely related to emphasis is directing the audience through a composition. By placing elements, such as lines, curves, or strategically repeated shapes, the marketer leads the viewer's attention from one section to the next. This visual theory creates a dynamic feel that subconsciously engages the viewer.

Pattern

Repetition of the elements in a layout can add rhythm and reinforce a brand identity. Patterns like shapes, textures, or colors can create a subdued background to add depth and draw the viewer into the main content.

Rhythm

When colors, lines, or shapes are repeated but arranged in a variation such as spacing or sizing, it creates rhythm. It makes a layout not only more captivating but also gives it a stronger feel than just a plain background or gradation.

Unity

A layout engages the viewer when all of its components work together to create a comprehensive design. It will give them the impression that the communication is comprehensive and not fragmented.

Variety

Unity is when all design elements work together, giving the overall composition a sense of completeness. However, too many elements can make a design feel dull. Designers introduce variety by contrasting the shapes, colors, sizes, and space to keep the design captivating while still ensuring that the parts relate to one another. This balance between unity and variety is crucial for an engaging yet coherent design.

IMAGE 10-3

AI Practicum | ChatGPT prompt: show an image of the balance between unity and variety

Engaging design guidelines

These seven rules, ranked in order of importance, will determine the success or failure of your project. Solve the problem, or it doesn't matter how good the design appears. If you have a stunning design that you believe other designers will admire, discard it. It may not be as exceptional as you perceive, and it would be beneficial to move past it in order to create something truly remarkable.

Inspiration to communicate the message

Create a mental and physical library of everything you see that is designed well—even if it is not the complete design but just a small portion.

Balance

If the finished design is difficult to look at, with no space to rest the eye and nothing fitting, then you failed as a designer. The space, graphics, images, and fonts need to visually work together.

Large, medium, and small create visual interest

Consider examining a design where all elements are the same size—where does your attention go, and why? Designing well is clearly not worth the excessive labor involved. Scale establishes a visual hierarchy.

Light, medium and dark tones to attract the reader

Your marketing product must initially attract attention, be visually appealing, and subsequently be memorable. Tones are effective; envision a uniform color scheme in which larger, bolder type appears darker than thinner, smaller type.

Use three fonts or less on a design

It is not necessary to employ an excessive number of typefaces solely because you have thousands of fonts on your computer. Reserve a portion for your subsequent design. This rule does not include a company logo, as it is primarily a visual element. Please bear in mind that a company logo is distinctive; if you employ the same font elsewhere, it will no longer be distinctive.

Typos kill a design

Clients, and anyone else who sees a word or phrase spelled incorrectly, are unforgiving of misspellings. Use a spell check and then read it out loud.

IMAGE 10-4

AI Practicum | Canva prompt: Show an image of a plane overhead pulling a banner that reads Marketing's workhorse is a flyer.

Why is a flyer a marketing's workhorse

The main goal of a client is to get as much of their return as possible within their allocated budget. Discussing the objectives of the flyer with the client and graphic artist is the most efficient strategy. These conversations should decide the flyer's size, color scheme, PMS options, overlap effect, and whether to print on both sides.

The highest cost of printing a flyer is the paper stock. Because leaflet fliers use thin, low-quality paper for pamphlets or circulars, they are usually low-budget print runs.

Before assessing the content, people unconsciously consider the paper's thickness and quality as a physical response. The likelihood that the reader will pause to examine the message increases with paper thickness.

The length of time the flyer will be on the press impacts the printing budget. A press's operational cost rises in direct proportion to its size, but it offers the advantage of allowing for the simultaneous printing of more pages.

While a 6-color press or higher can include PMS colors, a 4-color press can only produce CMYK. A digital laser printer that prints in CMYK format without PMS is an alternative that the customer may select if the print run is brief.

The standard flyer measures 8.5 by 11 inches (ca. 28 cm) and is in letter format. You can print the flyer on one or both sides, also known as a leaflet, sale sheet, or leave-behind. It is possible to print the flyer two-up horizontally on a page, which would make each flyer 5 inches (ca. 13 cm) wide by 8.5 inches (ca. 22 cm) tall, or 4.15 inches (ca. 11 cm) by 11 inches (ca. 28 cm) vertically. A bleed's area determines whether or not the size has an impact on the design.

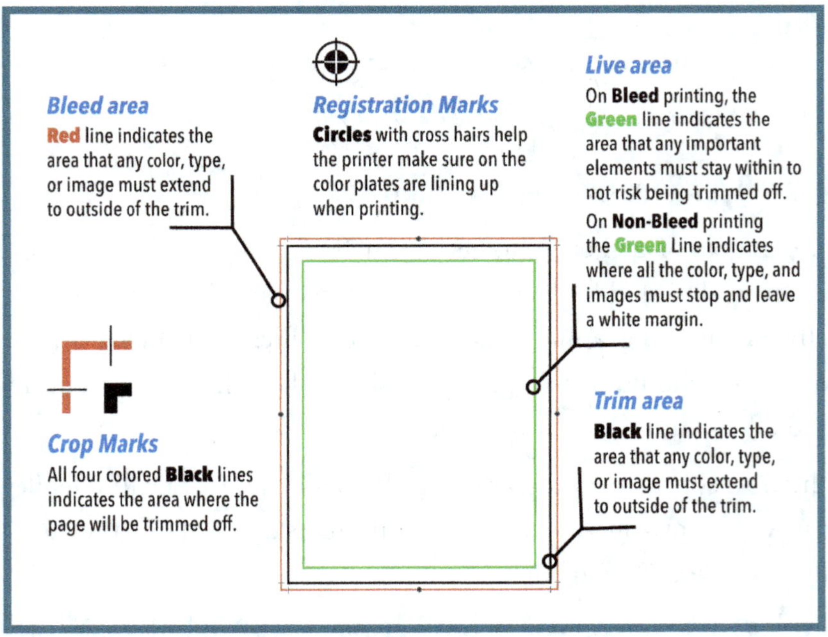

IMAGE 10-5

Diagram of flyer with bleed, trim, and safety margin.

Flyer mechanicals

Flyers are relatively easy to lay out. The difficult part is making them attention-grabbing. After you download the file that you created on one of the AI generators, you will need to send it to the printer. They will either print it on a copier machine or a printing press with a four-color process.

If the flyer has images or colors that go to the edge of the page, they need to extend past the trim. This way, when the flyers are cut down to size, there are not any white strips along an edge since trimming the pages is not a perfect process.

Furthermore, there is a live area on bleed printing for you to keep your important information within, so it does not get cut off. When you create a non-bleed flyer, you will need a white border around the edge of the flyer, and this area is called the margin. Any background color or images need to stay within this area. Depending upon your printer's specifications, you may need to add crop marks that show where the flyer trims and registration marks are that the printer will use to make sure all the colors are lining up and not giving you a double or triple image if the press plate is slightly off alignment.

Most printers will want the flyer in four-color process CMYK. Most AI generators create the projects to be printed in RGB. You will need to convert it with an application such as Acrobat to the four colors before sending the file.

Everyone's go-to answer

Flyers are an affordable alternative for businesses, particularly small and local ones, because they are generally inexpensive to print and distribute. Marketing uses flyers because they are versatile for reaching a large audience to promote goods, services, or events. They serve as a company's tangible representation.

A digital image on a screen elicits a different response from people than a real handout. It engages the customer and is tangible. The colors, graphics, and typefaces are more vibrant than they would be on a cell phone. The paper's weight conveys a message in a subtle way. Thin, light paper is inexpensive. The cost of glossy, thick paper is high. These qualities have the power to subtly evoke feelings about the company, service, or product. Flyers increase brand remembrance and engagement because people can hold, consider, and even save them.

These sell sheets can be tailored to a variety of marketing goals, from advertising sales or special events to promoting new products or services. Businesses can reach a certain market by distributing in high-traffic regions.

A comprehensive marketing strategy would use flyers with a broader message, as opposed to digital marketing, which can reinforce the flyer while focusing on all aspects of the market. The ability to disseminate a leaflet to other potential clients makes it easy to share.

A flyer with a white border is known as a non-bleed and will come with printer specifications. If the image appears to extend to the flyer's edge, it actually goes beyond the flyer and is trimmed.

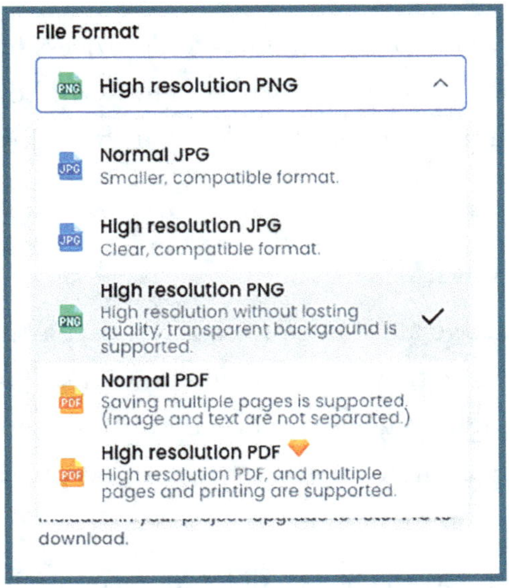

IMAGE 10-6

Screen grab of Canva download options.

Flyer creation with AI tools

Flyers are relatively easy to lay out. The difficult part is making them attention-grabbing.

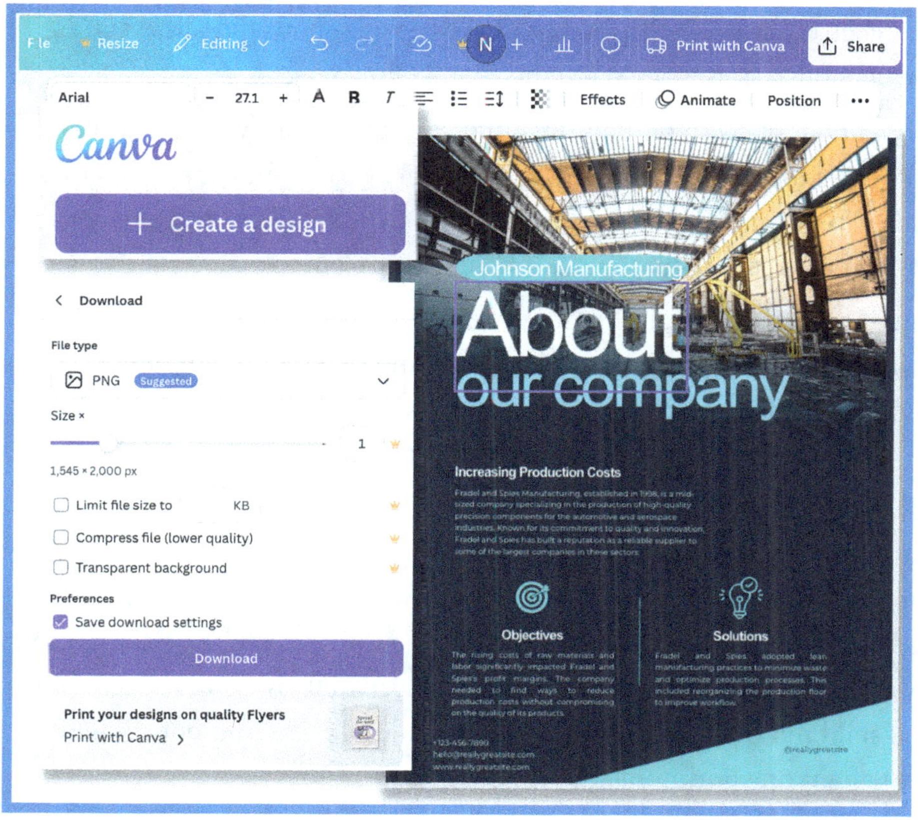

IMAGE 10-7

Canva toolbar, download options, and template flyer.

DEMONSTRATION **CANVA** FLYER

Select the "+ Create a design" button at the top of the panel (left on Mac and right on PC). In the search bar, type *flyer*. Select an orientation—portrait is vertical, and landscape is horizontal. Scroll through the templates and select one you can edit. It does not have to be perfect since the next step will give you a number of options. Once you select a template, you will be given more choices. You may also start with a blank canvas.

With your cursor, hover over areas of type and change the words. When you click on an area, the toolbar at the top will show and allow you to change fonts, sizes, colors, weights, and alignments.

A small bubble with options, including the three dots, will appear to allow you to make adjustments in real time. Be careful with safety areas for the type and visual margins. Many of the templates need someone with a design eye to fix the placement of the elements.

You have the option of choosing a size when you download; larger is always better. For instance, even though an 8.5"x11" document was chosen, the download default was 1545px x 2000px, which equals 5.5" x 6" when set up for printing at 300 pixels per inch, which is the standard for press printing.

Note your options are JPG or PNG files to download, which are great for internet elements, but most printers will require a PDF file. You will need 2550px x 3300px for a non-bleed flyer and 2625px x 3400px for a bleed flyer. Canva can save and download the flyer PDF as CMYK. The colors will shift and be less vibrant since they are using inks and not created using light on your monitor.

The Steps

Create Flyer: Search for "flyer" or a specific flyer type such as "business flyer," or "event flyer."

Choose a template

Edit Text: Click on any text box to edit the text, change fonts, sizes, colors, and styles.

Add Images: Upload your own images or use Canva's free stock photos, illustrations, and graphics.

Change Colors and Backgrounds: Modify the color palette and background to match your brand or event.

Utilize Canva's extensive collection of icons, shapes, and various design elements to enhance the visual appeal of your flyer.

Select "Download" to save it as a PDF, JPG, or PNG file.

If you want to print your flyer, you can order prints through Canva Print. Which has a button on the dropdown menu.

DEMONSTRATION **ADOBE EXPRESS** FLYER

To create a flyer with Adobe Express, start by opening the platform and choosing a flyer template. Explore Adobe Express's large template library of flyers, which are also set up in categories. If you prefer to start with a blank page, select the Create from scratch option.

Select the "Create New Project" button, if you want a quick start, and in the search field, type in flyer, event flyer, or hiring flyer, and then customize it with text, images, colors, and fonts to match your needs.

Edit your flyer template by selecting the content you want to change and using the type options on the toolbar. Use the Media selection to upload your own images or select from Adobe's stock images. Add icons, shapes, or other decorative elements from the "Elements" panel to enhance your design. Utilize the drag-and-drop editor to modify the size, rotation, and position of your elements. Use the built-in alignment options but keep it to one or two alignments.

In order to maintain a consistent layout, you may either implement an existing color scheme or develop a custom one that aligns with your branding.

Proofread and review your work before downloading. It is difficult at this time to really look at it with a fresh perspective, so if you can save and come back later, you have a better chance of catching typos and branding errors. One benefit of Express is that you can receive your flyer as a PDF once you are satisfied with the layout.

The Steps:

Select a new project and search for the type of flyer you want to design.

Use the text tools to add headlines, body text, and other information.

Upload your own photos or use Adobe Stock images.

Choose Colors and Fonts: Select colors and fonts that match your brand or desired aesthetic.

Add design elements by using shapes, icons, and other design elements to enhance your flyer.

Upload your logo and brand elements to ensure your flyer is brand-style consistent.

Save your flyer as a high-quality image or PDF by downloading it. You will need to convert it to CMYK before sending it to a printing press.

If you're in the US or UK, you can print your flyer directly from Adobe Express.

Export your flyer to social media, email, or your website.

DEMONSTRATION **PICSART** FLYER

Follow the link to picsart.com and then pick "Product ads" from the business section. The next step is to click the start button, then type "flyer" into the search area. After that, navigate to the drop-down menu that is labeled "Best for you ratio," and scroll down until you find "Flyer 8.54 X 11."

You can also edit the text, fonts, and colors, and apply filters and effects if you start with a template, like with other AI tools. For the purpose of printing, you can download an image with a high resolution. A paid membership is required for most modern and professional templates, and the flyer designs are not as professional as those created with Express or Canva.

IMAGE 10-8

Fotor original template poster.

DEMONSTRATION **FOTOR** FLYER

To create a flyer, go to fotor.com and select "Graphic Designer." Then select " "Flyer" or Poster" if you want more template options.

Select a subject such as "Hiring" and then select a template. The poster can be sized before downloading to flyer size.

You may want to generate that sales copy from a content provider such as ChatGPT or Gemini because the content that is available at the Pro level may not have the impact you need. You can download the flyer as a high-resolution PNG or PDF file, but to print it, you will need to convert it to CMYK.

With the AI generators, most of them provide an image in RGB that you need to convert to CMYK for a printing press. Converting the colors will cause the image to appear dull and less vibrant than they do on the monitor. There is software such as Adobe Photoshop that will have the ability to adjust the hue saturation after conversion. It will still not be as bright.

The Steps from Scratch:

Use your email or social account to log in and access design tools.

If you want to start from scratch, select AI tools and then AI Image Creator. If you want to start with a template, select Creator and, in the dropdown, select Flyer Maker; skip to Step 4.

Describe your flyer. You will need to try different adjectives in your prompt.

Customize the flyer after it is generated by selecting each element.

Click Download and choose the format. A high-resolution PDF will work the best, and this option will require a premium account.

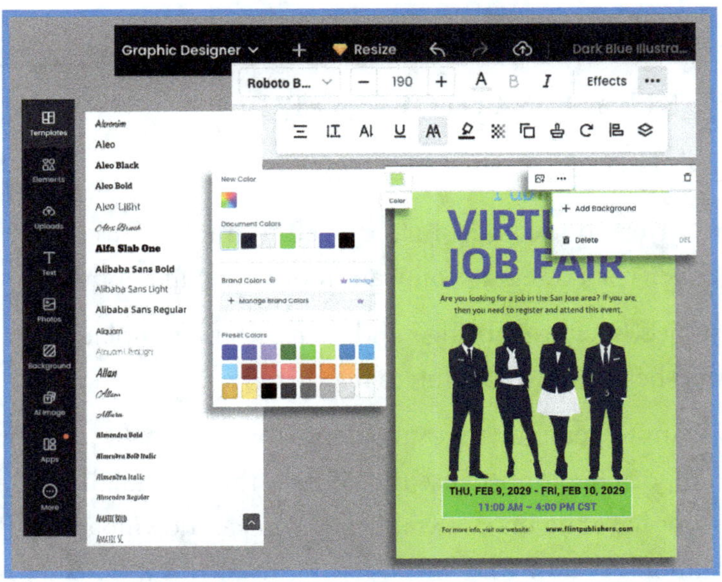

IMAGE 10-9

Fotor toolbar, download options, and template flyer.

Disclaimer

When using generative AI tools for creating images and designs, the results are generally available for commercial purposes. According to the US Copyright Office (see below), copyright ownership cannot be claimed for any of the images. AI-generated images may infringe on third-party intellectual property rights. Please review the "Generative AI Terms of Use" for any AI tools you utilize.

The US Copyright Office has confirmed that AI-generated material and suggestions are not protected by copyright. In its report, *Copyright and Artificial Intelligence, Part 2: Copyrightability*, the office concluded that "Copyright protects the original expression in a work created by a human author, even if the work also includes AI-generated material." Conversely, copyright does not apply to AI-generated content that includes some human content. The report clarified that from a graphic design standpoint, artificial intelligence is copyrightable if it is used as a tool to style or produce effects in human-generated work. For definitive guidance on your design, consult a copyright attorney. The report is available at: copyright.gov/ai/Copyright-and-Artificial-Intelligence-Part-2-Copyrightability-Report.pdf

Inspirational Ideas

11

Learning Objectives

The learner will change their view on design boundaries. They should be capable of diagramming a social post design approach. The user is expected to evaluate the impression of a marketing concept.

Think outside the comfort circle

Creatives will encounter the phrase "Think outside the box" during client presentations, signifying the client's disinterest in the design and lack of direction. Because it gives them a sense of security, they might feel more comfortable with the design concept they have seen elsewhere. It is possible that the designer presented an innovative concept that will be noticeable and draw interest. Conversely, the concept may be trite and not engaging. The basic idea is that we live in, drive in vehicles, and work within confined spaces. To create a distinctive and innovative design, we must step outside our comfort zones and challenge ourselves to discover the most effective layout for our clients.

Most marketing students want to immediately start with creating posts, marketing, and advertising. They have fantastic ideas and are ready to begin the fun part of creation.

They may have great ideas, but usually when they are assembled, the concepts are not quite as good as they pictured OR they only see the ideas and cannot step back to realize they are mediocre. A lot of ideas are just regurgitating what has already been done out there in the marketplace or rely on very cool images that do not sell the brand, service, or product. Strongly different imagery grabs attention.

For instance, what do you think this post is trying to sell or communicate?

IMAGE 11-1

When you use AI for your logo, you get what everyone else is using for a logo. So much of your budget is on branding; use a professional to create a unique and possibly trademarkable logo.

AI Practicum | Adobe Illustrator prompt: Create a house logo for a contractor.

Use your skills for good design

When you look at messages today on the internet or while driving, see if you can count how many times this solution has been used for roofers, home inspectors, Realtors, security firms, or even house lighting. This type of logo can be used for free or for a fairly low price, which makes you wonder how much the marketer or company owner values their brand.

Since you know how to use AI for design, this is a brief explanation of why you should use the tools for certain marketing projects but not the huge ones with overwhelming ramifications, such as the brand.

Companies spend a large portion of their budget building a brand.

Marketing relies on a well-designed logo and comprehensive brand. They should hire a professional to create a unique, eye-catching, memorable concept. Perhaps the business owner believes spending $25, the same price as a haircut, for someone to design a brand could seem like a reasonable price. They are ignoring the perceived value of their company by potential customers viewing and reacting to their logo. Business owners should pinch pennies in another marketing area. It would be better to save money on a marketing piece that has a short life so if it flops, it's not a big deal.

While there is an initial investment, hiring a professional can save time and money in the long run by avoiding costly mistakes and ensuring that branding materials are effective and efficient. Graphic designers possess the skills and expertise to create visually appealing and effective designs that align with a company's brand goals and target audience.

A well-designed brand can help a company stand out from the competition and create a unique and memorable impression on customers. It creates a positive first impression on customers, which is crucial for building relationships and driving sales.

There are numerous reasons to hire a professional graphic designer for the creation of a company's brand. Such a strategic investment can result in heightened brand recognition, enhanced customer engagement, and a more polished and memorable brand image, ultimately contributing to increased sales and long-term success.

A robust visual identity is essential for any company. A professional graphic designer can craft a distinctive and memorable visual identity, encompassing a logo, color palette, typography, and overall aesthetic that accurately reflects the brand's values and resonates with its target audience.

An effectively designed visual identity facilitates easy recognition and recall of a company by customers, leading to greater brand awareness and recognition. Branding materials such as websites, marketing collateral, and packaging that exhibit a professional appearance foster a sense of professionalism and establish trust with customers.

Competent graphic design captures attention while communicating messages and driving engagement, thereby improving marketing outcomes. A professional graphic designer ensures that all branding materials and communications maintain a consistent look and feel, fostering a cohesive brand image.

Although there is an initial expenditure, engaging a professional can save time and money in the long term by mitigating costly mistakes and guaranteeing the effectiveness and efficiency of branding materials. Graphic designers possess the requisite skills and expertise to create visually appealing and impactful designs that align with a company's brand objectives and target audience.

A well-crafted brand enables a company to differentiate itself from competitors, leaving a unique and lasting impression on customers. It also creates a positive first impression, which is crucial for establishing relationships and driving sales.

IMAGE 11-2

An abstract illustration showing that outside the comfort circle are unknown creative solutions.

AI Practicum | NightCafe prompt: An illustration of a round, medieval, fluffy, comfortable circular pillow that must be round lying on a rough and cracked concrete floor. The AI generator kept showing square pillows until the word "round" was repeatedly used in the description.

Value of not following the herd

There are a number of books on guerrilla marketing that are filled with crazy concepts. The term refers to developing ideas that might sound outlandish, are not expensive, and will get attention for your business.

For example, in 2001, Taco Bell announced they would give everyone in the U.S. a free taco if the Mir space station hit a floating target placed in the South Pacific. That created a buzz. Virgin Airlines offered high-top sneakers with built-in Wi-Fi for everyone that flew first class.

Everyone has ideas on marketing, so as a business owner, see which ones you are doing and rate how they are doing with regard to bringing in old and new customers. The first thing to analyze is your marketing literature. If you know someone that is a mentor or knows design, ask them.

If your budget is limited, check with the local college's graphic design and marketing schools to see if they have a class where the students apply what they have learned and get to work with a real business. Your materials will take a while to be ready, most likely a semester, but if they're free and eye-catching, then you win.

You will hear a lot of people talk about a blog, but if you do not have many followers, use your limited time on what gets results. Update your website with a fresh look showing some of the gatherings at your open house events. Your Google Business profile needs to be updated and used to announce open houses and new home listings with photos.

Think about your networking group, chamber of commerce, and PTA or Rotary. Design different postcards to hand out at these meetings. With AI generators, you have the ability to make flyers directed at different markets. They can be printed off on heavy paper from your personal computer.

Besides putting a sign in a customer's yard when you are working on their house, drop off the flyers you made in Chapter 10 and collect names and addresses for mailers. Use Adobe Express or Canva to create a homeowner's guide for your networking group that could contain contractors, financial advisors, emergency numbers, and local restaurants that the network members could hand out to their clients.

Update your website with a fresh look showing some of the gatherings at your open house events or a high-speed video of a project from start to finish in thirty seconds. Use Google Business to upload videos and photos. Chapter 13 goes into a few of the AI tools that make videos for posting.

Inspirational case studies

The following inspiration ideas are to demonstrate other ways to approach a post. They are not too detailed and are only to get your creative ideas flowing.

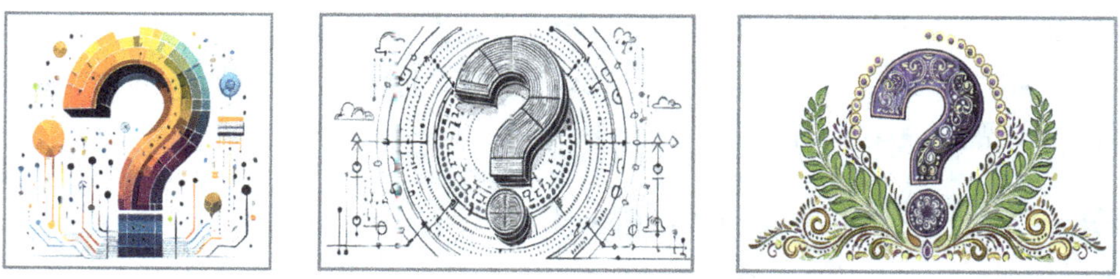

IMAGE 11-3

An abstract illustration showing that outside the comfort circle are unknown creative solutions.

AI Practicum | Adobe Illustrator prompt: An illustration of the question mark.

Inspired Idea #1: Ask a question in your post

It may not receive as many likes or overall engagement, but questions in posts receive more comments than brags and announcements. To begin a dialogue with fans, ask questions or pose business questions to find out interest in a new product or service that you may be considering. For the questions, the person at the business who is responsible for posts should generate the questions to keep the voice consistent and timely. Individuals will not keep checking for a response.

Respond to comments and start new threads to show you value your audience's input. Retail brands can boost post comment rates by using "question" posts, which generate twice as many comments despite slightly lower overall engagement.

Although retail brand Wall Posts that include questions receive slightly lower overall user engagement in terms of 'likes' and comments, this type of post generates more than double the number of comments compared to "non-question" posts.[1]

Individuals like to talk about themselves —every good salesperson knows this. In a post, you could pose questions about their favorite way to unwind after a long day, the movies or TV shows that impressed them, or if there is a hobby or a skill they would like to learn.

Business-focused approaches could ask about a favorite benefit they found with your product. You may ask a follower about your posts and what has been their favorite topic has been. You could have fun and pose an off-the-wall question such as, If your product or service had a theme song, what do you think it should be?"

Inspired Idea #2: Realtors® sell the sales feature

Look at posts by Realtors®, and most of them are the same. There is a photo of the front of the house, sometimes inset with small pictures of the inside and the description with a call to action to contact the agent with their info.

IMAGE 11-4

AI Practicum | Adobe Express prompt: Entryway of house with an 1800s-style large crystal chandelier, maximalism style.

When our Realtor® walked into our beautiful house that we were putting up for sale, she told us how nice the leaded glass windows were, and our paint colors set a nice tone for each room. Then she recommended that we change the entryway chandelier. I thought the one we had looked great, but we listened and changed it out. The Realtor® was right. The buyer commented at closing that when she saw the chandelier, she knew that was the house for her. The Realtor® featured the chandelier in online listings and in posts. She made our house stand out. It had great curb appeal, as did many competing properties. I did not see any with a nice chandelier in the entryway.

Realtors®, especially the ones who have experienced the highs and lows of the market, know how to sell. They will tell you they know how to market, but how do they know? Because they are still in business? Maybe their success is because they have established a strong network or referral system. For many, I have found that their marketing is the same process as the last ten years; only now it involves even more social posting.

As in any business, you need to know how the competition is doing. Most Realtors® know membership in the National Association of Realtors® has dropped the last few years.[2]

The Realtor® marketers who research the industry and realize that a number of home sales agents are dropping out know that means less competition for them, and they need to decide how they can take advantage of this with buyers and sellers. Develop a USP in your marketing to stand out.

Further research into the industry studies the sales outlook. Mark Palim, Fannie Mae Senior Vice President and Chief Economist, said, "Due to the ongoing lock-in effect and affordability constraints, we currently expect another year of sluggish existing home sales."[3]

Inspired Idea #3: Foundation Repair is all about the USP

One of the fastest-growing home foundation repair companies that I know of has an interesting sales pitch. I was speaking with the owner about how they had broken into the market with a sales process they constantly tested and refined. Then she confided in me that what had really made them a success in this market was their USP.

The market differentiator that impressed potential customers was to show their competitor's pier and her company's pier. The sheer size discrepancy made it an obvious decision. She went on to explain the differences and the features but just showing me the two foundation piers was more than enough to sell me. After putting piers under their homes, no one wants to do it again.

To stand out from competitors in social media and direct marketing, a company needs to know what makes it unique. Such an approach allows marketing to highlight its strength and set itself apart in a crowded market to increase sales and customer loyalty.

Remember there are no degrees of being one of a kind when choosing your company's USP. It is either unique or not. A well-defined USP establishes a strong brand identity by clearly communicating the company's value proposition and drawing in customers seeking those benefits.

This allows the company to tailor its marketing messages, advertising campaigns, and overall strategy to highlight that key selling point, ensuring a clear and consistent message to the target audience. As a marketer, your goal is to establish a strong brand identity. Customers are more likely to buy when they comprehend the value.

Probably the most obvious method to find out your company's strongest selling point is to ask customers why they chose them. This method allows you to create content that resonates with your ideal customers.

Another option is to ask the salespeople what selling proposal excites customers the most. There will usually be more than one answer. By defining the strongest selling point, you can use it as the foundation for the overall business strategy.

A third option is to state the problems your product or service solves and narrow it to the top benefit. This strategy strengthens customer connections by showing the organization knows the customer, their needs, and a solution.

Having a unique selling proposition (USP) is crucial for successful marketing, as it prevents you from wasting your efforts on less impactful messaging. A campaign with a main selling feature can attract the right audience, maximize conversions, and build a strong market presence.

Inspired Idea #4: Fill in the blank is more than a game

One of the most engaging post techniques is one of the most underutilized. Data indicates that brand posts implementing the "fill in the blank" approach, such as "I like ___________," generate comment rates that are nine times higher than those of other post strategies. Less than 1% of retail brands are utilizing this strategy, even though the data shows it is a proven approach exclusive to the retail sector. You can introduce each of these questions with your own answers.

For the post: The #1 reason I live here is ____________________.

Your answer: I live here because it is a vibrant community that fosters friendships and connections among its members.

For the post: My go-to vacation place is ____________________.

Your answer: A secluded beach is my go-to vacation spot, where I can unwind and escape the bustle of daily life.

For the post: If you could customize our product in any way, what would you change? ____________________.

For the post: What problem did our product/service help solve?

____________________.

Inspired Idea #5: Partner with like-minded businesses but not your competition.

The owner of a growing floor installation company developed relationships with plumbers, roofers, home inspectors, and painters. Instead of always posting about his support of local charities, he can also post with a fellow contractor at community events, and they can reciprocate. That is a good way to increase the number of followers and present interesting posts.

Together they could have a social media competition on shares and give the winner a free carpet stretching, have a room painted, or have a kitchen faucet replaced. It does not have to be a large giveaway item. The idea's novelty will get you noticed. The posts can lead up to the big event, and you can make a video of whatever is won and installed.

Inspired Idea #6: Run a completion contest

Consider offering more than discounts in your post advertising—offer a prize for the most shares. Another option is to offer something you supply that does not cost the customer more.

As an example, a carpet installer could offer a professional foot massage to everyone who bought new carpet. His customers might not buy from him solely for that reason, but it could capture their attention. By providing added value, you can position yourself as the local small business owner while encouraging customer loyalty and referrals through unique incentives.

Inspired Idea #7: Have a video with children playing

A number of businesspeople have told me about their social engagement successes with their children or grandchildren in their videos. During the filming, the children were having fun, and something unexpectedly hilarious occurred. This approach is as splendid as the goofy pet tricks because people are drawn to them and share the videos. Just post it with your logo and contact info.

As an example, if you sell bed mattresses, create a video showing kids jumping up and down on your mattress and giggling. Then give a short explanation about the mattress quality. Keep it short; even though Facebook and YouTube want longer videos, your audience will most likely tune out after 14 seconds. At the end of the video, have your child playfully hit you with a pillow, and you could offer that as a free item—the pillow, not the hit.

Viewers spend an average of one to three seconds on a social post, but videos can get up to eight seconds.

1| Bullas, J. (2024, August 24). 10 Powerful Tips to Increase Fan Engagement on Facebook. Jeff's Jabs. https://www.jeffbullas.com/10-powerful-tips-to-increase-fan-engagement-on-facebook/

2| LaTrace, A. J. (2025, January 3). NAR membership dips below 1.5M—Will losses continue? Real Estate News. https://www.realestatenews.com/2025/01/03/nar-membership-dips-below-1-5m-will-losses-continue

3| (2025, January 22). ***Higher Mortgage Rates Likely to Keep Existing Home Sales Near Multi-Decade Lows***. Fannie Mae®. https://www.fanniemae.com/newsroom/fannie-mae-news/higher-mortgage-rates-likely-keep-existing-home-sales-near-multi-decade-lows

Hints and tips

12

Learning Objectives

The student will be prepared to interpret how color affects the viewer. The reader will be qualified to demonstrate AI generative marketing apps. They will be able to figure out with AI a schedule for social media posts.

Email tips

Email marketing remains an effective promotional instrument for products and services. It is easily quantifiable with potential consumers as a personalized and targeted marketing piece. Emails are an effective approach to maintaining communication with current clients. On each campaign, the marketer must evaluate the results of the various email messages to determine which approach resulted in higher conversion rates and enhanced customer engagement. It is a cost-effective method for establishing brand awareness, driving sales, and reaching a large audience as long as it is measured. If the emails are sent out with the goal to bring in sales, it is not very effective and most likely will lead to a SPAM rating for the sender.

To start, determine the type of email you are crafting and maintain consistency with that narrative. For example, prospecting emails are those types of sales emails in which the salesperson reaches out to a potential customer. This important message about the product or service sets the tone, reflects the company, and builds the brand.

If the email serves as a follow-up to maintain customer engagement, please ensure it is personalized. How many times have you received a happy birthday email from a company that you are unable to remember minutes after reading the beginning sentence? People know these messages are automated and now AI-generated.

Email return addresses should have a name and not be generic. Emails like info@, customer service@, and sales@ are impersonal, often tagged as spam, and end up in the junk folder. Choose an address that conveys a friendly and approachable sender. Please ensure that the domain part of the address matches the company's URL. This consistency enhances credibility and helps recipients easily recognize the source of the email. Additionally, personalizing the subject line can further increase the likelihood of your message being opened and read.

Customer retention importance

Jack Werner, PhD, has repeatedly informed his mentees, "The easiest customer to get is the one you already have." Most people receive too many emails because for a business it is easy and cheap. Send out a handwritten note. You can use AI to write them. Send out a text. You can use AI to send them out in bulk but make them look personalized to the past customer. Call them. There are AI voicemail services that let you record a message and then send them in batches to past clients to make sure they are still pleased with your product or service.

Social posting hints

Make everything you communicate to a past or potential customer interesting. Decide if you would want to read it or if you would pass over it. Everyone is busy and does not have time for anything but their family and business. Actually, this is only what they think; individuals really have free time, but they do not want to waste it.

Viewers like to look at pictures of people. Since they were infants, humans have been attracted to faces. This was validated in 2014 in a study of Instagram posts. "…the study shows that Instagram pictures with human faces are 38 percent more likely to receive likes than photos with no faces. They're also 32 percent more likely to attract comments."[1]

However, subsequent studies have found the opposite. Individuals want to see images where they can imagine themselves in the scene or using the product instead of someone showing how to use it.

Make them quick reads or videos. Individuals will not spend much of their time reading a novella or watching a feature-length documentary. The shows with short videos of entertaining and simple imagery work best.

IMAGE 12-1

Example of a design with space and color to attract readership. Notice the bottom line consists of many elements that, as a group, are centered to provide a base for the layout.

AI Practicum | ***Creator*** *prompt: Ad for financial advisor showing someone living on an island.* ***Express*** *to create a flyer with this verbiage: Relax. You are financially comfortable.*

Sales literature secrets

When creating on a computer, it's easy to overlook the basics. To draw a potential customer's attention, employ large, medium, and small items to provide contrast. Color appeals to readers. Black and white graphics fade into the surrounding literature and appear cheap. Adding a second color to a black-and-white design can be more successful than using full-color graphics.

Keep plenty of space around any type. Avoid turning your message into something where the reader has to sort through the content to figure out what you are communicating. Do not make it seem like work. Your message should be clear, short, and easy to understand.

Instead, aim for a clean and organized layout that allows the text to breathe. This approach enhances readability and ensures that the key messages stand out, making it easier for potential customers to engage with your content.

Use AI to help manage your social media posts

Buffer is a flexible social media management tool that leverages AI to optimize post scheduling. The app analyzes your audience's engagement patterns and suggests the best times to post. Buffer's AI also provides insights into content performance and recommends improvements to increase your reach and engagement. Only has paid plans.

Hootsuite is a powerful and popular social media management tool that uses AI to enhance your social media strategy. Its AI-driven features include post scheduling, content curation, and performance analytics. Hootsuite's AI suggests optimal posting times and identifies trending topics, helping you stay relevant and engage with your audience effectively. Pricing has a free version and paid plans.

PostPlanner is designed to help you plan and schedule posts with maximum efficiency. Its AI algorithms analyze your past content performance and audience engagement to suggest the best types of posts and optimal posting times. Post Planner also offers a content discovery tool, helping you find trending topics and viral content to share. Pricing has a free version and paid plans.

SocialBee is a social media management tool that uses AI to help you schedule and recycle content. Its AI-driven features include post categorization, optimal scheduling, and performance analytics. SocialBee ensures that your content remains fresh and engaging, even as you reuse successful posts. Has only paid plans.

Tailwind is a social media management tool with specialized features for Pinterest and Instagram. Its AI-powered SmartSchedule feature suggests the best times to post based on your audience's activity. Tailwind also offers content creation tools and performance analytics to help you optimize your social media strategy. Only has paid plans.

Set up a workflow

There are a number of steps where a workflow will be beneficial. To market your company, you should have a step-by-step system in place that you follow. It will save you time and help with the scheduling.

Step One —Strategy

Define your marketing objectives, including brand awareness, lead generation, and sales goals.

Identify your target market demographics and research relevant trends in your industry. Research and define the ideal customer profile.

Make notations on how your competition is marketing. This is a good time to brainstorm general content ideas to achieve the goals and medium that would have the best chance of success.

Decide on the focus of key themes and topics, but do not get too specific at this stage. Build a budgeted list of all the costs and hired assistance and allow for unforeseen changes. Identify the methods for measuring the success of each part of the campaign.

Each task should have a person responsible for following through. This person is the champion of that specific part of the campaign. They will be in charge of the decisions that will be faced for that element to be ready and put into motion.

IMAGE 12-2

AI Practicum | Picsart prompt: Create a calendar with people and papers and computers flying around it.

Step Two — Schedule

Set up a timeline with a calendar with reminders and a spreadsheet with checkboxes and dates of the content distribution. This calendar should show all of the elements in the marketing campaign so you can see how things coincide and build to a final date. It will need a schedule for all your marketing communications, such as social posts, sales flyers, and emails. Include the timeframes to produce the elements.

The spreadsheet should have individual tabs for the specifics of each medium in the campaign. Use automation tools to put the different elements into the process.

Do not forget to set up a communication portal to keep everyone updated on each other's progress. If it is in the budget, use collaboration tools to allow teams to work together in real time on different tasks of the campaign.

Social posts should have posting dates, the platforms, and content formats such as text, images, and videos with due dates and whether they have been proofed and are ready to post.

Printed material dates start by counting back from the in-hand date to include mailing time, production time, approvals, and proofing.

Step Three — Creation.

Develop content pillars that can be adjusted for each target market and medium. List each marketing element, such as web articles, posts, flyers, and postcards. Include content and graphics to be used and the status. Audience engagement needs to include communication responses to comments and replies.

Step Four—Analysis.

Track KPIs, (Key Performance Indicators), with monitoring tools. Make adjustments if the data is not being collected correctly. Depending on the marketing goal, indicators could refer to increased revenue attributed to marketing, the number of prospected qualified leads, website traffic increase, or social media engagement.

After everything is set up, if time allows, have a proof-of-concept run-through. Make notes on the areas that did not work or had problems so you can go back at the end of running the scenario. After beta testing the campaign, have one final run-through.

The successful workflows are simple steps for building a marketing campaign or project. Depending on the breadth of the campaign, there may be a lot of moving parts, but focus on keeping task descriptions short.

Improve posts with AI content research tools

BuzzSumo is a content research tool that uses AI to identify trending topics and high-performing content in your niche. By leveraging BuzzSumo's insights, you can create posts that resonate with your audience and tap into current trends. The tool also offers influencer identification, helping you connect with key figures in your industry.

CoSchedule Headline Analyzer indicates how effective your headlines are for quality metrics and provides suggestions to improve them. It is very useful for SEO, and the results are AI-driven analyses of competitors content. The prompts will help you generate and improve ideas with feedback. {Details: Free.}

See your design clearly.

You think you are designing on a computer that will show you the truth. But it will fill the screen with your design, which clearly means what you see is not what you will get. The monitor may show 100%, but that does not refer to the actual size of your design — it refers to the resolution on the screen. This will cause you to think the type and images are large.

If you are working on a leave-behind (see Chapter 8), measure the trim size. If it is supposed to be 8.5 inches, but on the screen the trim is 10 inches, you will need to reduce it. For instance, I know my main Thunderbolt monitor needs to be at 81% to be actual size. If I did not adjust the percentage, think how large my type would be and how very little space would be left for the design.

If you are working on a Facebook post, open Facebook on your computer and on your mobile device. Measure a post. Now adjust your screen to the actual size. On my monitor, that is 68%.

Purchase a clear ruler and measure the page size on your screen and compare it to the specs. Adjust the software's magnification to the actual size the final piece should be so you can clearly see the scale of the elements.

If you do not adjust your sizes, do not be surprised when the elements are too large or too small. By the time you see your posts, it will be too late to adjust.

Combating message overkill

A marketer's job is to catch the interest of the audience so that they want to read the content. Although it may appear easy, viewers often ignore the majority of the more than three thousand messages sent daily to targeted consumers, making it all the more important to design a visually appealing solution. Because of the growing popularity of digital tools, the majority of designers jump straight to the program in an effort to come up with novel concepts. In contrast, imaginative designers conduct research first, then generate thumbnails, and lastly produce a comprehensive layout in an effort to provide a unique design that captivates readers.

Marketing messages may not get actions, but if they are viewed, then they are not complete failures. If a target audience is not interested in your company, they will bypass the post. But they may remember the brand for when they do need your company, and then that is half the battle. If that is achieved, it leads to future sales, and while that is difficult to measure, the communication was a partial success.

By knowing the target market, the designer can make informed decisions and revisions such as font choice, colors, and the overall content. These visual artists examine the thumbnails to discover whether there is another way to grab the viewer's attention, rather than jumping to the computer and laying out a design they picture in their minds. Making a headline with images and coming up with a unique idea can be a powerful marketing tool.

Marketing artists need to see things in a bigger picture. The more references a designer has, the better they can connect with all ages, jobs, and lifestyles. They will be able to develop a message that's effective.

Do some research first. When designers start their work on the computer and come up with an idea, they almost never come up with five different ones. Inspiration can strike at any time. If you want to make thumbnails, you should have blank paper, detailed notes, font choices, and color palettes close at hand.

Space for all

Clients will contend that information ought to fill every available space. They will request the enlargement of specific elements, subsequently raising the size of further components to emphasize a particular point. If an experienced visual artist fills the entire space, the message could lose its attraction.

An excellent layout incorporates margins that establish a frame surrounding the design. Although margins need not be uniform, many individuals perceive symmetrical margins as more aesthetically pleasing. A design may stretch text to an image or a color block; however, the graphic artist should refrain from reaching the page's edge.

Novices often struggle with comprehending and exploiting wide areas because they design on a computer and rarely print their work to examine it in full size. Contrast serves as the primary factor for captivating viewers, and space is undeniably the most critical ingredient required to establish contrast.

Do not undervalue design space. A marketing artist will design to create an illusion of greater space and fewer elements to distract from the message.

Successful messages lead the eye to the prize

Hierarchy in design refers to how you want the viewer's eyes to read the message. If the design makes it difficult for the viewer to figure out the information, the marketing will not be successful. If the elements are placed haphazardly, not only will the communication be a failure, but the reader will also move on to another, more inviting message.

1| Maderer, J., Bakhshi, S., Gilbert, E., & Shamma, D. (2014). Face It: Instagram Pictures With Faces Are More Popular. *Georgia Tech.* https://doi.org/W911NF-12-1-0043

AI Motion marketing for social media

13

Learning Objectives

By the end of this chapter, the student is in a position to develop social posts with animated videos. They will be capable of differentiating the basic editing tools. The reader will be competent to appraise the success of a social media post.

Quiet your mind

As a creative, your mind will be brimming with various ideas, visuals, and strategies for marketing a company or product. Throwing out the average, overdone ideas and the concepts that are so far-fetched that the viewer cannot comprehend them in three seconds of casual reading is the most challenging step.

Before you start listing all your ideas, compile a list of the reasons why your business is the preferred choice of your target consumer. Consider taking notes on this consumer, including their demographics and, most importantly, the advantages that your company offers that your competitors do not. This understanding will help you tailor your message effectively, ensuring it resonates with potential customers. By emphasizing these unique selling points in your marketing campaigns, you can create a compelling narrative that differentiates your brand and captures the attention of your audience.

Next, write it down in giant characters on a Post-it note and stick it to the screen of your computer in a prominent area. The number of words should be between seven and nine. Be certain that your ideas address that main feature of the selling point.

Focus on how you can show the audience the value of your product or service. Your company's strongest argument to a customer must be visual superiority. Many businesses rely on reviews and five stars to prove their value. A video, recorded and edited correctly of a real customer explaining why your business is the best will be the strongest argument you can show on your website, in a post, in an online ad, and in email campaigns.

IMAGE 13-1

Example of thumbnails for a UFC & Century Martial Arts Fight Night commercial.

Practicum | For your video, sketch out how you see your video unfolding with short notes on each side.

Videos have advantages over text in that they will increase trust, create an emotional connection with the viewer, and prove to the target audience your product or service is wonderful.

In contrast to written testimonials or generic marketing text, hearing and seeing actual consumers talk about their experiences fosters authenticity and trust. Video testimonials make the message more memorable and persuasive by allowing viewers to share the customer's excitement and feelings.

Video captures attention and improves message retention because it is naturally more entertaining than text. These testimonials are an effective kind of social proof because they show how your product or service has a real-world impact.

Ready, action!

Before you start generating the video, get ready with a timeline and description of your video. Create thumbnails by drawing stick figures and notations using a pencil and a blank sheet of paper. Begin by attaching one thumbnail to your timeline for every five seconds of footage that you have. You should include notes on how you see the film moving and what types of images will appear and slide off the screen. If you have photographs, you should place them on a page in thumbnail size.

Capture the attention of your target market in the first few frames. Make sure your branding is clearly presented, and you end with a call to action and a link to a landing page and telephone number.

Research the various special effects choices that could be compatible with your idea. You need to make a decision regarding whether you will develop 3D graphics, such as Claymation, or 2D animated graphics and text to achieve rapid alignment with your personnel or customers. Ultimately, the choice between 3D and 2D animation will depend on your project's goals and the emotional impact you wish to convey. Consider how each option can enhance your storytelling and engage your audience more effectively.

Choose an AI generator

Research video AI generators. Every month, more options with different pricing are available. Besides the ones listed in the demonstration sections, there are many paid and free options to choose from. Artlist.io has a wide variety of styles with no limit on video lengths. It has a 20GB size limit. Synthesia generates 6-second videos at a resolution of 720p. OpenAI, the company behind ChatGPT, developed Sora. Sora can make up to 60-second videos. Renderforest is known for its animation videos.

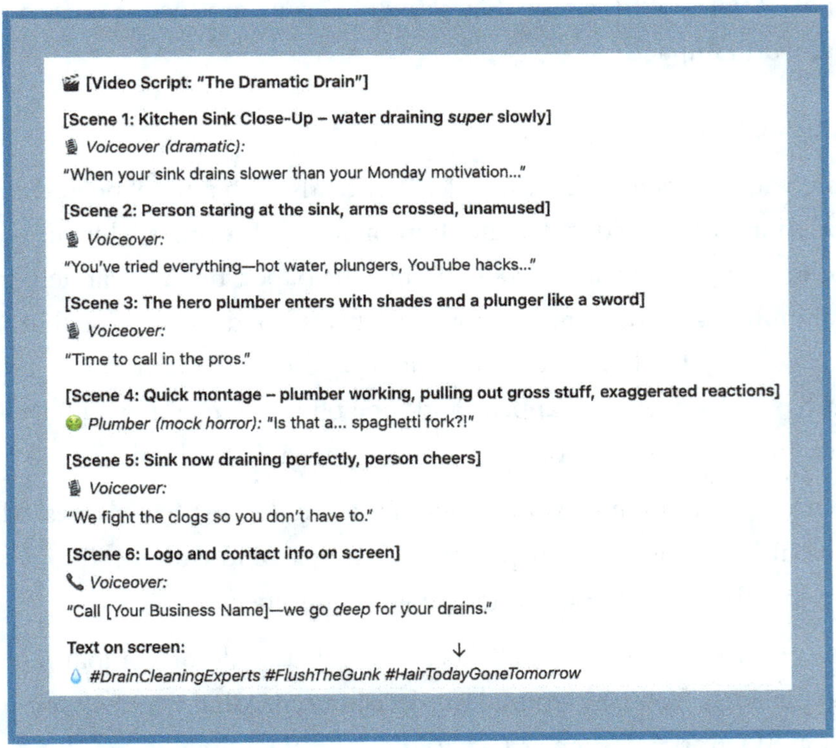
🎬 **[Video Script: "The Dramatic Drain"]**

[Scene 1: Kitchen Sink Close-Up – water draining *super* slowly]

🎙️ *Voiceover (dramatic):*

"When your sink drains slower than your Monday motivation..."

[Scene 2: Person staring at the sink, arms crossed, unamused]

🎙️ *Voiceover:*

"You've tried everything—hot water, plungers, YouTube hacks..."

[Scene 3: The hero plumber enters with shades and a plunger like a sword]

🎙️ *Voiceover:*

"Time to call in the pros."

[Scene 4: Quick montage – plumber working, pulling out gross stuff, exaggerated reactions]

🤢 *Plumber (mock horror):* "Is that a... spaghetti fork?!"

[Scene 5: Sink now draining perfectly, person cheers]

🎙️ *Voiceover:*

"We fight the clogs so you don't have to."

[Scene 6: Logo and contact info on screen]

📞 *Voiceover:*

"Call [Your Business Name]—we go *deep* for your drains."

Text on screen:

💧 *#DrainCleaningExperts #FlushTheGunk #HairTodayGoneTomorrow*

IMAGE 13-2

ChatGPT screen grab #1.

AI Practicum | ChatGPT prompt: Describe what would be a funny Facebook video post narrative for a plumbing company.

Video length: 30 to 60 seconds

Facebook accepts videos that are 240 minutes long, but that may not achieve the marketing goal of reaching more of the target audience. It is likely that viewers will not watch it repeatedly or share it. Within the realm of video, one of the most important markers of success is the length of time that individuals spend watching it, often known as the video retention rate.

> 🚽💥 *"Your Toilet Called. It's Tired of Taking Crap from Everyone."* 💥🚽
>
> We get it—plumbing problems aren't exactly dinner conversation. But when your sink starts burping or your toilet decides to become a fountain, it's time to call in the pros. 💦🛠️
>
> Just this week, we rescued a family from a rebellious garbage disposal that thought it was a wood chipper. True story. 😂
>
> At [Your Business Name], we fix leaks, clogs, drips, and those mysterious noises that keep you up at night. No mess, no drama—just solid work and a few bad plumbing puns along the way. 😎
>
> 📞 Call us before your plumbing stages a full-blown mutiny: (123) 456-7890
> 📍 Serving [Your Area] with good vibes and better wrenches.
>
> 🚿 Hot water? We got it.
> 🚽 Backed-up toilet? Consider it handled.
> 😬 Awkward questions about your pipes? We've heard worse.
>
> #FlushTheStress #CallThePlumber #PipeDreams #WeKnowOurSh*t

IMAGE 13-3

ChatGPT screen grab #2.

AI Practicum | ChatGPT prompt: Try a humorous approach for the drain cleaning narrative for a Facebook post.

The social media platform Facebook recommends that films and tales that are less than one minute in length or clips that are less than twenty seconds in length are more likely to generate viral engagement.

If you're eager to qualify for in-stream ads, it may help to extend your viewing time. Videos must last more than three minutes to be considered for the competition. This length requirement allows creators to showcase their storytelling skills and engage viewers more deeply. As a result, investing time in crafting longer videos can ultimately enhance your chances of reaching a wider audience and maximizing your impact.

Additionally, Facebook recommends that videos be longer than three minutes in length when it comes to the creation of tales, live streaming, or serial series.[1]

DEMONSTRATION ADOBE **CHATGPT** VIDEO SCRIPT

ChatGPT was prompted to develop a 30-second Facebook video ad. GPT really likes to put emojis all over the place, so when you see them on emails, you will know where they came from. The result was very long and complicated, so the prompt was shortened, and ChatGPT was directed to write a 5-second video ad.

After trying a number of approaches to get the correct wording, it delivered a pretty good script. Unfortunately, except for Visla, it was too detailed for most of the AI video generators.

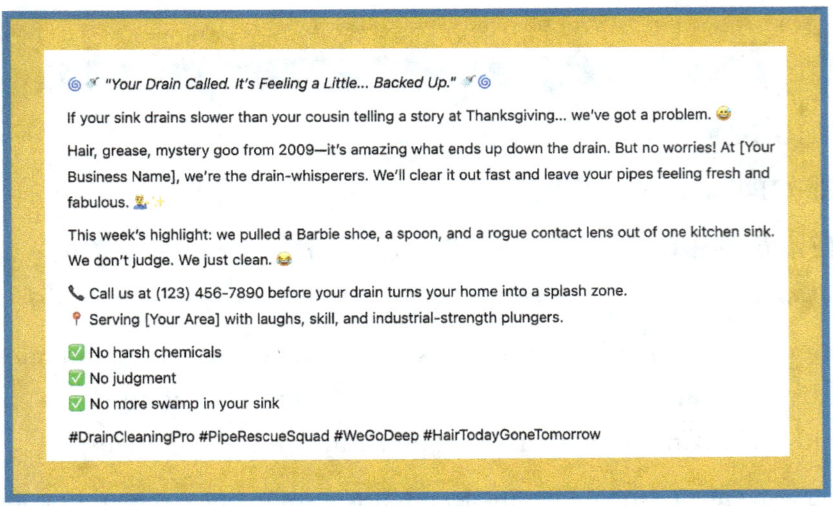

IMAGE 13-4

ChatGPT screen grab #3.

AI Practicum | ChatGPT prompt: Try a little less humor for the funny video ad for the drain-cleaning narrative Facebook post.

🎬 **[5-Second Script: "Drain Drama"]**

[Scene 1: Sink gurgling, water not draining]

🎙️ Voiceover (mock dramatic):

"Your drain is crying for help..."

[Scene 2: Plumber pops in, winks, clears the drain]

🎙️ Voiceover:

"We answered."

[Scene 3: Sink drains perfectly – logo + contact info on screen]

🛠️ Text: *[Your Business Name] – Drain Cleaning Pros*

🧼 Hashtag: *#FlushTheGunk*

Image 13-5

ChatGPT screen grab #4.

AI Practicum | ChatGPT prompt: Shorten the script to 3 seconds.

DEMONSTRATION ADOBE **FIREFLY** VIDEO CLIP

Firefly is limited to 5-second videos, and it is an excellent artificial intelligence tool to learn how to create a video because it is straightforward to use. Strong and maximalist imagery is present in it. In the event that you possess an editing program, you have the ability to combine clips. This feature allows for greater creativity and flexibility, enabling users to craft more engaging content. Additionally, the ease of combining clips means that even beginners can produce polished videos with minimal effort.

In Adobe Firefly, you have the option of beginning the process of creating a movie with either a text prompt or an image. When using text-to-video, you should compose a comprehensive prompt that describes the scene, the action, and the style. Upload an image and describe the movement you want to achieve when using the image-to-video feature. The next step is to create the video and then modify it by modifying settings such as the aspect ratio, camera angle, and motion. These adjustments will allow you to fine-tune the final product to match your vision. Once you're satisfied with the result, you can export the video and share it with your audience or use it for further creative projects.

IMAGE 13-6

Firefly screen grabs from script based on ChatGPT. Options on inset.

AI Practicum | Firefly video prompt: Scene 1: Sink gurgling, water not draining. Scene 2: Plumber pops in, winks, clears the drain. Scene 3: Sink drains perfectly.

First, go to the Adobe Firefly website and select "Generate video." Enter a text prompt in the prompt field. Write a descriptive text prompt (up to 175 words) that includes details like shot type, character, action, location, and aesthetic.

As an option, you may want to upload an image to use as the first frame. Set the aspect ratio and frames per second, then choose the shot size and select the camera angle. Decide on the camera motion. In the Advanced section, use the Seed option to control randomness. Text prompt to guide the AI on how to animate the image. Finally, select "Generate."

Explore other options by regenerating with similar variations. Try special effects such as a lens flare, water, or smoke.

Positives

Dynamic images work the same as creating an image.

Different eye-catching animated images.

Fast download speed.

Negatives

Limited to a 5-second video clip.

No audio.

If you do not upload an image, it will create an animation as shown in Image 13-2.

DEMONSTRATION ADOBE **EXPRESS** MOVIE

Express technically does not have any time limit for videos; nonetheless, it is important to take into account the amount of time it takes to make and download videos. When you are ready, you have the option of either making a video from scratch or using a template. Using the tools that are offered, such as trimming, cropping, and creating transitions, you may input your media, including movies, photographs, and audio, and then edit them. Once you have finished editing, you can preview your video to ensure it meets your expectations before finalizing the download.

Additionally, Express provides options for sharing your completed project directly to social media platforms or saving it in various formats for personal use.

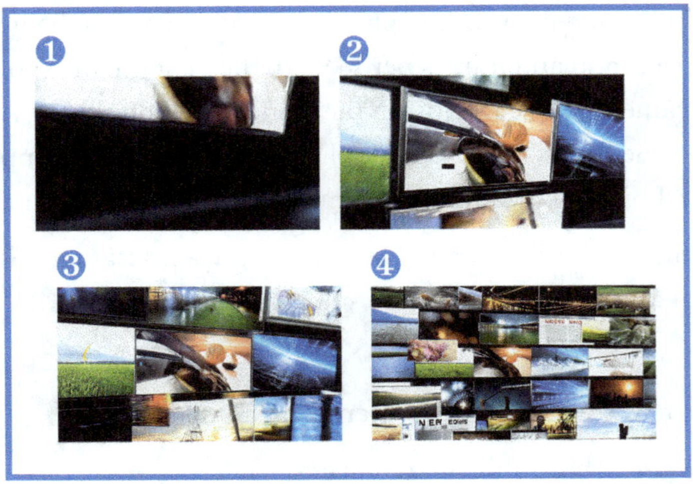

IMAGE 13-7

Express screen grabs.

AI Practicum | Express video prompt: Video montage of news, sports, and TV shows zooming into views and shrinking to allow more videos.

You can upload images and your own videos and use existing stock videos as a template.

See the steps for Firefly before proceeding. Some of the differences are that you have more editing functions, such as trimming and cropping the clips and adding transitions and audio. Audio will make your video file size much larger. Export as an MP4 file.

Positives

Dynamic images work the same as creating an image.

Different eye-catching animated images.

Fast download speed.

Negatives

Limited to 5-second clips.

No audio.

If you do not upload an image, it will create an animation as shown in Image 13-2.

IMAGE 13-8

Express screen grabs.

AI Practicum | Express video prompt: Video of fireworks. Steps: adding content over the fireworks video and adjusting fonts, color, alignment, and placement.

Exported as an MP4 with a resolution of 1920 x 1080; file size was 15 MB.

IMAGE 13-9

Visla screen grabs.

AI Practicum | Visla video prompt: Scene 1: Sink gurgling, water not draining; audio: Your drain is calling for help. Scene 2: The plumber pops in, winks, and clears the drain; audio: We answered the call. Scene 3: Sink drains perfectly! Audio and text: Call Plain Plumbers at 555-555-1212.

DEMONSTRATION **VISLA** MOVIE

With reasonably priced options, Visla appears to work better than many that were tested. Navigate to visla.us where you can try it out or log in and set up an account.

Scroll down until you come to the generator. Enter text into the field and select "Generate Video." It will take some time for the video to be ready for you to view. Do not close the browser window since it will stop producing the video. You can save the video to edit later or download it.

There are desktop apps for Mac and Windows clients and ones that work with your phone camera.

Positives

Real video of people.

Voice-over.

Closed caption.

Music track.

Negatives

Long generation time.

The free trial does not let you download.

Video requirements for social media

Videos (see site for complete requirements)

YouTube video:

Size/Resolution (Width x Height): 1920 x 1080 pixels

Length: Varies depending on the type of ad

Max file size: Less than 256 GB

File type: MPEG-2 or MPEG-4

Snapchat video ads

Size/Resolution (Width x Height): 1080 x 1920 pixels.

Length: 3–180 seconds

Brand: Up to 25 characters with spaces

Headline: Up to 34 characters with spaces

File type: mp4 or mov

TikTok video ads

Size/Resolution (Width x Height): 1080 x 1920 (portrait) or 1920 x 1080 (landscape)

Length: 5 seconds to 16 seconds

Max file size: 500 MB minimum

File type: mp4, mpeg, mov, or avi

Facebook video ads

Size/Resolution (Width x Height): 1440 x 1440 pixels.

Length: 1–241 seconds

Brand: Up to 150 characters with spaces

Headline: Up to 27 characters with spaces

Max file size: 4 GB

File type: mp4, mov, animated gif

1 | McLachlan, S. (2022, August 2). Ideal Length of Social Media Posts: A Guide for Every Platform. *Hootsuite*. https://blog.hootsuite.com/ideal-social-media-post-length

Secrets of the trade

14

Learning Objectives.

The reader will know how to incorporate free fonts that appeal to the target audience. They will be able to defend the importance of readable and legible fonts. The student of design is going to be in a position to explore which AI generator tool works best for a particular project.

Best source for assistance

Technology has put many answers to our questions and problems right in front of us. But searches only give answers to your questions quickly without going deeper or elaborating in ways that can be beneficial to you. A great source of information is the library. Many creatives will not want to go looking through books, but if you ask a librarian, not only can you get answers, but they will also ask your questions to give you what you are really looking for instead of what you asked.

At a library AI workshop, Goblin Tools was presented, which will list the tasks and subtasks, including a timeframe with milestones. This AI-powered tool can be used to break down a marketing campaign into steps for scheduling.

As an example, when prompted to estimate the tasks, including a timeframe to publish a book, it came back with 15 tasks and about that many subtasks. It would take about 212 days and 1 hour to research, write, edit, prepare the book for publishing, set up the eBook, and distribute it. If you are familiar with Kanban boards, these tasks fit perfectly into a 5-stage process.

Alegreya

Crimson

Literata

PT Serif

Shippori

IMAGE 14-1

Serifs for headlines and text.
Alegreya (12), Crimson (6), Literata (16), PT Serif (4), and Shippori Mincho (5)

Google has free fonts for designs

Google has over 700 fonts that appeal to your audience that are available, are free to use, and can be downloaded onto your desktop. The fonts are open source, meaning they are available for use without a license, and they can be used across all mediums as well as be used for personal modifications. It is a very wide selection from handwritten to clean sans-serifs. The styles span the whole spectrum.

There are millions of fonts to choose from for marketing which makes it difficult to choose the correct face. Typefaces that are interesting, very strong, and stand out should be used for headlines. Body text typefaces that have different weights and not an intricate structure are perfect for reading. For reading typefaces, multiple choices in weights and italic (serif) and slant (sans serif) allow you to stay within a family but emphasize words. You can get more content into less space if you use a condensed typeface but make sure the condensing does not lead to readability issues. The (12) after a typeface name refers to how many weights and styles are available in the family.

Every marketer and business owner should understand how a font's design sends a message to the reader. Choice of type is weighing the need for something that stands out with the desire that the typography be easy to read and help the message be memorable.

Bodoni Moda

Caudex

CINZEL

Judson

Noto Serif Display

IMAGE 14-2

Serifs for headlines.
Bodoni Moda (12), Caudex (4), Cinzel (6), Judson (3), and Noto Serif Display (18).

Crimson Text

Lora

Libre Baskerville

Merriweather Serif

Neuton

IMAGE 14-3

Serif for text.
Crimson Text (6), Lora (8), Libre Baskerville (3), Merriweather Serif (8), Neuton (6).

Alegreya Sans

Lato

Oswald

PT Sans Narrow

Open Sans

IMAGE 14-4

Sans serifs for headlines and text.
Alegreya Sans (14), Lato (10), Oswald (6), PT Sans and Narrow (6), and Open Sans (12).

Anton

BEBAS NEUE

Cabin Condensed

unica one

Outfit

IMAGE 14-5

Sans serifs for headlines.
Anton (1), Bebas Neue (1), Cabin Condensed (4), Unica One (1), and Outfit (9).

Albert Sans
DM Sans
Manrope
Onest
Rethink Sans

IMAGE 14-6

Sans serifs for text.
Albert Sans (18), DM Sans (18), Manrope (7), Onest (9), and Rethink Sans (10).

Type layout tricks of the trade.

Beginning designers will center the content. This alignment functioned for the first hundred years of graphic design, and it is safe if it has space and creates no problems for the reader.

The length of a paragraph should be manipulated for the reader. If it is more than 150 words, it may not be read. Paragraphs with more than eight sentences will be skipped over more than one with three sentences.

More than five lines of content become difficult to read when centered. A person will struggle to follow the content and find the beginning of the next line. When they become frustrated, they will move from one page to another.

Designers face challenges in three primary areas when addressing a problem: typography, color schemes, and spatial arrangement. Experienced designers do not depend on guesswork regarding typography. The selection of a font is a deliberate and considered choice. The principal role of typography is to convey a message, such as documenting an event, alerting to a weather change, addressing a political rally, or instructing from a textbook. The communication specifies the font family.

When a page is overflowing with text, the designer may choose a condensed font to reduce the amount of space and give the impression of less text to read. Individuals typically show reluctance to reading a lot of text. An alternative is to increase the number of pages or to condense the information into fewer words.

The absence of serifs and the lack of uniformity in the stroke weights of sans serif typefaces for body content can be a challenge for many readers. The serifs in an old-style font can enhance its readability but give the impression of being out of date. People grow up reading upper and lowercase and when presented with body content and long headlines that are in uppercase the target audience will skip it.

Reversed type, which is a light font on a dark background, can be difficult to read. Paragraphs of italic or script fonts can be difficult to read in print. On a monitor, reversed-out type may not be as difficult to read. Uneducated designers will use display type as body content not knowing it was never designed to be text, so it is too small and difficult to read.

Readable and Legible

Type readability refers to how the font design and structure influence the reader's ability to quickly comprehend the message. In paragraphs and long subheads this is an important aspect for viewers remembering the message. Legibility refers to how a font makes the message noticeable and understandable which is important for headlines and calls to action.

Headline vs. Paragraph

The most noticeable text on a marketing piece is the headline. The design should draw in potential customers and offer a quick overview of the content. Increase its prominence by choosing a bold, noticeable typeface or surrounding it with white space. The writing should be straightforward, convincing, and to the point. Occasionally a subhead with less bold and a smaller font size is required when delivering additional information. Since it includes the information, a potential customer needs to make a decision, read on.

The body text is the most crucial section for marketers. The choice of typefaces can significantly affect the design's tone and legibility. The designer must make sure the font is readable and keep it from being confusing by using more than three different typefaces. Condensing the body content with bullet points or short paragraphs helps improve reader engagement.

An overview of the artificial intelligence content, image and schedule generators

As with any technology, there will have been updates since this book was written. In AI, the advancements are on a fast elevator. Every day, artificial intelligence generators go online that are free, have free trial periods, and most have subscriptions. It is highly recommended you try them out for different marketing projects before signing up. Check out their resolution and size for print and internet use. Free versions usually have limited features with the subscriptions having levels of users and features.

LEGEND

Access	Cost Rating	Degree of Use Difficulty	Functionality	Resolution Use
F = Free	$	√+ = Very Easy	U+ = Many Features	Rp = Printing *
T = Trial	$$	√ = Easy	U = Average Features	Rw = Web
S = Subscription	$	√- = Difficult	U- = Limited Features	

* High resolution but download may need RGB to be converted to CMYK for Printing

All-In-One AI Generators

AI	URL	Features	Cost Rating		Use	Func.	Res
Express	express.adobe.com	writing, images, social posts, ads, flyers, logos.	F	--	√	U+	Rp
Canva	canva.com	writing, posts, websites, marketing	F	$	√+	U+	Rp+
Figma	figma.com	writing, posts, websites, marketing	F	$	√	U-	Rp+
ChatGPT 4.0	chatgpt.com	writing, posts, websites, marketing	--	$	√+	U+	Rw
DeepAi	deepai.org	writing, posts, websites, marketing	F	$	√	U	Rp
Picsart	picsart.com	branding, images, social posts, ads, flyers, logos	F	$	√	V	Rw
Pixlr	pixlr.com	images, social posts, ads, flyers,	T	$	√	U	Rw

Image AI Generators

AI	URL	Techniques	Cost Rating		Use	Func.	Res
Firefly	firefly.adobe.com	colorful, maximalist style art and photo		$	√-	U-	Rp
Craiyon	craiyon.com	multiple image styles and solutions	F	$	√-	U-	Rw
Creator	bing.com/images/create	simple compositions, minimalist style art and photo	F	$$	√+	U-	Rw
Fotor	fotor.com	images, social posts, ads, flyers, logos		$	√	U+	Rp
Nightcafe	creator.nightcafe.studio	Multiple image solutions in different styles	F	$$	√+	U	Rw

LEGEND

Access	Cost Rating	Degree of Use Difficulty	Functionality	Resolution Use
F = Free	$	√+ = Very Easy	U+ = Many Features	Rp = Printing *
T = Trial	$$	√ = Easy	U = Average Features	Rw = Web
S = Subscription	$	√- = Difficult	U- = Limited Features	

* High resolution but download may need RGB to be converted to CMYK for Printing

Content AI Generators

AI	URL	Cost Rating		Ease of Use	Functionality
Gemini	gemini.google.com	F	$	√+	U+
Copilot	copilot.microsoft.com	F	$	√+	U+
ChatGPT 3.5	chatgpt.com	F	--	√++	U

AI Schedulers/Planners*

AI	URL	Features	Cost	Rating	Use	Func.	Export
Goblin	Goblin.tools	Plan with times all tasks and subtasks, export, app	F	--	√	U+	Yes
Claude	claude.ai	writing, posts, websites, marketing	F	$$	√+	U+	No
ChatGPT 3.5	chatgpt.com	general timing and tasks, download timeline spreadsheet	F	$	√+	U	Yes

* Apps available for Apple and Android

Video AI Generators

AI	URL	Features	Cost	Rating	Use	Func.
Firefly	firefly.adobe.com	translations, creations, from image, 5 sec, no audio	--	$$	√-	U-
Express	express.adobe.com	video creation, generation from image	F	--	√+	U+
DeepAi	deepai.org	video creation, generation from image	--	$	√	U
FreePik	freepik.com	video creation, generation from image	--	$$$	√+	U+
InvideoAi	invideo.io	video creation, generation from image	F	$$	√	U
Visla	visla.us	video creation/editing, desktop and mobile apps	T	$$$	√	U+

Functional Image Editors*

AI	URL	Features
Home Designs AI	homedesigns.ai	Interior design
Idea Spectrum	ideaspectrum.com	Landscape design
Galaxy Ai	galaxy.ai	house-plans

* Not covered in this publication

Index

D

E

F

G

P

Q

R

S

T

U

V

W

Y

www.ingramcontent.com/pod-product-compliance
Lightning Source LLC
LaVergne TN
LVHW052324200926
848481LV00002B/665
* 9 7 9 8 3 4 9 3 1 3 9 4 3 *